Foreword by Governor Jerry Brown

The

ORANGE COUNTY FAIR

A History of Celebration

CHRIS EPTING

THE
History
PRESS

Published by The History Press
Charleston, SC 29403
www.historypress.net

Copyright © 2015 by Chris Epting
All rights reserved

First published 2015

Manufactured in the United States

ISBN 978.1.62619.802.9

Library of Congress Control Number: 2015939216

This book is dedicated to the millions of people over the last 125 years who have enjoyed the Orange County Fair, along with all of the hardworking people who make the fair possible each year.

CONTENTS

Foreword, by Governor Jerry Brown   7
Acknowledgements   9
Introduction   11

1. 1890–1920   17
2. The 1920s   38
3. The 1930s   44
4. The 1940s   50
5. The 1950s   61
6. The 1960s   76
7. The 1970s   86
8. The 1980s   92
9. The 1990s   98
10. The 2000s   107
11. Voices from the Orange County Fair   118
12. Some Final Facts and Figures   129

Index   141
About the Author   144

FOREWORD

Throughout the history of California, fairs have played an important role in the celebration of community.

From a three-day festival in 1890 to a twenty-three-day event with more than 1.3 million guests, the Orange County Fair has brought joy and special memories to millions of fairgoers for 125 years. The Orange County Fair has solidified its importance to the community by celebrating the rich agricultural history of the area and the accomplishments of the people of Orange County and California.

As you celebrate the significant milestone in the Orange County Fair's history, I send my best wishes for a memorable, educational and festive fair.

—GOVERNOR JERRY BROWN

ACKNOWLEDGEMENTS

Special thanks to the staff of the OC Fair & Event Center who contributed their time, photos, information and stories. Thanks also to Chris Jepsen and Steve Oftelie at the Orange County Archives for their images and information. I would also like to thank Patrick and Peggy O'Donnell for their time and images, as well as Jim Bailey and Becky Bailey (Findley) for their time and stories. Additionally, thanks to writer and Huntington Beach city historian Jerry Person for his remarkable pieces on some of the earliest Orange County Fairs. Finally, thank you to my wife, Jean; son, Charlie; and daughter, Claire, for their support and patience. As always, I am indebted to my family.

INTRODUCTION

A n article appeared in the *Los Angeles Herald* newspaper in 1892, just two years after a certain fair had begun in Orange County, California. Already it was calling it an annual fair. Did the paper have any idea of where it would all go?

THE ORANGE COUNTY ASSOCIATION ANNOUNCE COLT STAKES

The directors of the 32ᵈ district of Orange county announce the following colt stakes to be trotted and paced at the annual fair. No. 1—Three-year old trotting stake for foals of 1889, and eligible to the 3:00 class. Best 2 in 3, mile heats, to harness; $100 added by the association. No. 2— Two-year old trotting stake for foals of 1890. Best 2 in 3, mile heats, to harness; $75 added by the association. No. 3—Two-year-old pacing stake for foals of 1890. Best two in three, mile heats, to harness; $75 added by the association. No. 4—One-year-old trotting stakes for foals of 1891. Best two in three, mile heats, to harness, one hour between heats; $50 added by the association. No. 5—One-year-olds—One-year-old pacing stakes for foals of 1891. Best two in three, mile heats, to harness, one hour between heats; $50 added by the association. Entries close March 10th, when the first payment is to be made. The payments are in easy installments. Entry blanks containing conditions and all other information can be obtained by addressing W.A. Beckett, Santa Ana.

INTRODUCTION

The *Los Angeles Times* detailed in 1979:

> *Shortly after Orange County was formed, in 1889, the Orange County Fair Corporation was formed. There was no fair as such in 1890, but the newly incorporated group sponsored a horse race in Southwest Santa Ana and put up some fair exhibits in the French building. It wasn't an extremely active group, since a second group got underway in 1894. It was when the second group of men tried to form the Orange County community fair corporations they discovered the name already been taken. State law prevented a second organization from taking the name for 50 years. Not to let a good idea go to waste, the group renamed themselves the Orange County Fair Association, Incorporated, and began to plan for annual fairs.*

And plan they did. Back in 2014, I wrote a preview article in advance of the opening of Orange County Fair. It was a fairly simple and short piece just to offer a brief description of the path the fair had taken over the course of almost 125 years:

> *One of Orange County's most venerable traditions returns this week. Celebrating its 124th year, the Orange County Fair has charmed, dazzled and delighted millions of people over the years with rich traditions that go far beyond deep-fried Twinkies and bacon-wrapped everything.*
>
> *In its earliest incarnation, back in the 1890s, it was a quaint community fair that didn't even last a week. There were no food vendors nor carnival rides; simply some livestock exhibits and even a horse race.*
>
> *Over the years it hopped around the county, from Anaheim to Santa Ana and (during World War II) to Huntington Beach, until eventually settling in Costa Mesa in the early 1950s.*
>
> *For all of its Midwest trappings and classic fair touches, the Orange County Fair also boasts several homegrown finishes that have become touchstones of this vaunted event.*
>
> *For one, there is the recognition of special Orange County residents who've made a positive difference in the community. They are celebrated each year with special ribbons and awards.*
>
> *Then of course there is the Centennial Farm, the centerpiece of the agricultural area of the fair, celebrating the deep roots of Orange County. Centennial Farm is an actual three-acre working farm that was created to provide educational opportunities regarding agriculture for visitors. Chickens, cattle, goats and other farm animals all call this*

Orange County Fair 1949   Fair Site

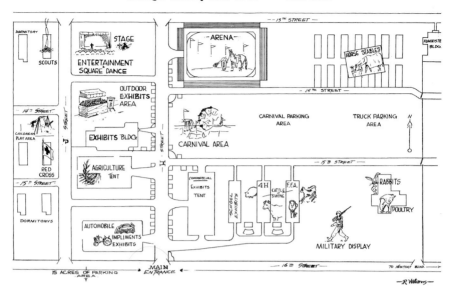

A 1949 map of the Orange County Fair. *Courtesy Orange County Fair archives.*

home and can be easily viewed while walking through the lush and fragrant gardens.

For folks that love fair food, here are some interesting facts from 2014, as reported by the fair:

- Chicken Charlie used 7,500 gallons of vegetable oil to fry up 24,000 bacon-wrapped pickles; 100,000 deep-fried Oreos; 25,000 balls of his top-selling deep-fried cookie dough; and other wild concoctions.
- Biggy's Meat Market sold nearly 2,000 "Big Chics on a Stick" and 4,500 "The Big Ribs;" and used 13,500 pounds of potatoes for orders of giant "Curley Frys."
- Bacon-A-Fair used 20,000 pounds of bacon around turkey legs, inside chocolate, wrapped around cheesy bombs or sprinkled around chocolate peanut butter bananas.
- Tasti Chips used 23,750 pounds of potatoes and 690 gallons of cheese sauce.
- Juicy's sold more than 75,000 smoked turkey legs, and used 300 gallons of ketchup and 250 gallons of mustard.

This year, the theme is "Summer Starts Here," and from July 11 until August 10 you will be able to enjoy one of the most festive and

Garden Grove exhibit with Pat Locker of Fullerton High School. *Courtesy Orange County Archives.*

Orange County Fair exhibit, August 1949. *Courtesy Orange County Archives.*

Courreges Ranch Display, Orange County Fair, August 1949. *Courtesy Orange County Archives.*

authentic county fair environments in the country. Historical, hysterical and everything in between—the Orange County Fair is a must-visit summer attraction.

In my head, I knew that I was working on a more comprehensive story about the fair—this book. Over the course of the next several months of researching and opening old boxes in the archives to go through programs, the ribbons photos and other artifacts, I truly start to get a sense of just what makes the fair so special. In these modern times, of course, people always seem to get fixated on the outrageous food and rides at the fair. But as I was reminded, both by researching and talking to lots of people connected to the fair, to truly experience the heart and soul of this event, you have to go see the livestock...and learn about the agriculture...and spend time perusing the exhibit halls. I think those were always my favorite things at the fair anyway. But like many people, in the last few years I probably did start getting hung up a little bit on the other things. That's normal, I suppose. Fairs are supposed to have exciting, loud, colorful and tasty attractions. But as big and bold as this fair gets, thankfully it has never forgotten what got it there in the first place. In those quieter spaces or hearts beat faster at the thought of receiving a blue ribbon or watching your livestock go up for auction. That's where the Orange County Fair really lives.

So, by all means, the next time you enjoy the fair, wander, fill up and take it all in. But don't forget to experience the true magic of any good county fair. It's in the pans and it's in the soil.

In the meantime, I hope you enjoy this overview of each fair aspect over the years—the themes, the events, the performers and more. It's a scrapbook of sorts, culling stories, newspaper articles, firsthand accounts and other resources to present a collection of the many things that have taken place over the years and, of course, to celebrate this most notable anniversary of 125 years.

Someday I think it would also be worthwhile to create a compilation just of people's observations and memories from the Orange County Fair. Do you have any you'd like to share? We'd look forward to hearing from you. In the meantime, let's go to the Orange County Fair.

Chapter 1

1890–1920

A fair is most commonly thought of as "a gathering of people to both display and trade produce and other items while also parading and displaying animals." The essence of the fair is that it is a temporary thing, sometimes lasting one day and sometimes lasting months. Fairs are actually an ancient tradition that go all the way back to early Rome. Throughout the Middle Ages, fairs became important as places for wholesale trading, and they were often tied to religious holidays. In the nineteenth century in the United States, fairs became very important in terms of promoting state agriculture—competitions featuring livestock and farm products became not just popular but integral to the development of agriculture. This was long before games, rides, concerts and food became part of the equation.

Beginning in the early 1800s, the first agricultural fairs gave rural families an opportunity to see firsthand the latest agricultural techniques, equipment, crops and livestock. Over the course of the nineteenth century, fairs also incorporated a wide range of other activities. As much as the culture changed, the agrarian education and competitive programs continued to be at the heart of any community fair.

The very first state fair to take place in the United States happened in 1841 in the upstate community of Syracuse, New York. The second state fair began in Detroit, Michigan, back in 1849. Within the next few decades, the popularity of fairs and the need for them started taking root all across the country.

A 1920s image from the Valencia Orange Show. *Courtesy Orange County Fair archives.*

So begins our story in Orange County. Just for some historic perspective about what period in American history we are talking about, in 1891 Thomas Edison patented the motion picture camera, the radio and the two-way telegraph. Two years later, the Ferris wheel was built by George W. Ferris at the World's Fair in Chicago. One year later, in 1894, Coca-Cola was first sold in bottles. Henry Ford built his first car in 1896; also that same year, electric lights were used for the very first time at the state fair.

In 1889, the Orange County Community Fair Corporation was organized shortly after Orange County was formed. They were destined to grow with each other, intertwined and reflecting each other's values and experiences for decades.

What can be considered as the very first Orange County "fair" took place in 1890 at a Santa Ana racetrack then located at Bristol Street and Edinger Avenue in Santa Ana. The track was a one-mile oval, and the horse races that year featured famed racehorse Silkwood, who won a $1,500 purse over McKinney, then reputed to be the fastest horse in Los Angeles County. But the event wasn't just a horse race. The Orange County Community Fair Corporation also put up some simple exhibits in the French Opera House building near Fourth and Bush Streets. The four-day event took place October 7–10.

In 1891, a second group called the Orange County Fair Association was formed and took over the reins of organizing the fair. Judge J.E.E. Pleasance was president. For the next several years, until 1894, the fair was continually held both at the racetrack and the French Opera House. And Silkwood was still making appearances that drew plenty of spectators.

Here are a few items from June 1892 in the *Los Angeles Herald* newspaper that detail some events at the fair that year:

TWO BIG PURSES OFFERED BY THE ORANGE COUNTY ASSOCIATION

The Herald *has received a program from Secretary Beckett for the third annual meeting of the Orange County Fair Association. The program is a very ambitious one for a town of the size of Santa Ana—probably the best ever offered in the west with a town of less than 500 people. The fair begins Tuesday, September 27th, and ends on Saturday, October 1st. Interested parties can get programs upon application to Secretary Beckett, Santa Ana, Cal. There is a flavor of originality about the directors of the Orange County Association. For instance, in the trotting and pacing races, a horse not winning one beat in three is sent to the stable.*

A LARGE ATTENDANCE

Roy Rex and Frank M. Win the Trotting Races. Santa Ana, Sept. 27.—The third annual fair of agricultural district No. 3 opened today by races and exercises in the evening at the pavilion. The horticultural and agricultural displays are the finest ever seen in the county. In the morning, mile dash, Princess First, won first money; Prince Second, and Hank Johnson third. The purse was $250, and the time 1:45.

The trotting race for 3 minute horses for a purse of $300, had four starters, and Roy Rex won the first and second heats in 2:32⅞, and 2:28⅞. The third heat was given to Roy Rex, Conn coming in first, but losing the heat on account of breaking badly. Time, 2:28⅞. Conn got second money. In the trot for Orange County horses, in the 2:50 class, Frank M won the two first heats in 2:48; Glen Fox second, Maggie F third. The attendance was large.

In 1895, the fair was moved completely to downtown Santa Ana, near Fourth and Bush Streets. Neal's Hall was added as a fair exhibit building, and Silkwood's abilities as a racehorse began to wane, thus resulting in smaller crowds for the fair.

By the next year, Silkwood was no longer appearing in the racing at the fair. Several other well-known horses were recruited to appear, but none of them had the magical Silkwood appeal. Still, the fledgling fair had made enough of a name for itself to continue on.

Although reports are scant from the end of the century, there are still tantalizing notes that remain. By 1897, the fair had incorporated several more agricultural exhibits and livestock exhibitions and was held in Santa Ana October 27–29. One newspaper account reported that there was a large barbecue tended by Dan Marco Forster for the opening of the 1897 fair. The menu included barbecued beef, freehold eight, carne asada, bread and costillas (beef short ribs). Horsemen and horses from all of the coastal area competed in races, and there was even a Lady's Day on October 27 at which all women were admitted for free.

By the early 1900s, American agricultural fairs had evolved into major productions featuring processions of many animals, bands, displays of local industries and artisans. Women were attracted to participate by offering premiums (cash prizes) on domestic entries and by holding an annual ball. New clubs and organizations such as 4-H and Future Farmers of America were formed and helped build programs of support, education and continuity in the agricultural society of the United States. That's why, in the early 1900s, the Orange County Fair hired a publicist who would meet with exhibitors months before the fair and submit stories to the local papers about the efforts to gin up interest in the annual event.

The more the public experienced the concept of a county fair, the more people seemed to embrace it. By 1902, there were seventeen traveling carnival troupes operating across United States. Within several years, that would grow into the hundreds.

A HISTORY OF CELEBRATION

From 1903 to 1910, it is not known precisely where the Orange County Fair migrated. Again, many details are scant from the earliest days of the fair, but it is believed to have remained in Santa Ana. It is known that in 1906, the fair was named the "Parade of Products" and was held in conjunction with a celebration of the completion of the Pacific Electric Railway from Los Angeles to Santa Ana. Included in the celebration was the completion the Balboa Pavilion in Newport Beach, along with a host of floats and products representing Orange County. The name "Parade of Products" became "Carnival of Products" in 1907 and would grow to include more street parades throughout Santa Ana, featuring wagons loaded with the largest and best produce in the area.

That year, 1907, the very first carnival queen, Ms. Ethel Chapman, daughter of C.C. Chapman, the "Valencia Orange King," was crowned. (Chapman had grown rich in the county growing and packing his Old Mission brand oranges). The tradition of having a fair queen became an annual event until 1983—hopeful contestants would interview, pivot and pose in both evening gowns and swimsuits, vying for the coveted crown.

In 1910, the parade was located in Anaheim at the intersection of Clementine and Cypress Streets right near well-known Pearson Park. There,

The Anaheim Carnival Queen and her court, circa 1912. *Courtesy Orange County Fair archives.*

in 1911 and 1912, it was dubbed the "Anaheim Carnival." By this time, refreshment stands had begun springing up all over the fair to meet the needs of the crowds, and new prize competitions were established for livestock, produce and homemaking skills. The Carnival of Products had become a smash hit, its popularity paralleling the continued growth of Orange County.

In 1913, the fair moved out to San Bernardino, where it existed as part of the National Orange show, which took place February 17–22. By all accounts, there were no fairs held from 1914 to 1916 due to World War I.

By 1917, the Orange County Fair was back in business, only now it had moved to the beach for the first time. Once again a fall festival, November 23–24, the fair was held in Huntington Beach in four large tents near the intersection of Yorktown and Main Street, the present site of today's civic center. Dubbed the "Harvest Home Festival," within a year it would become the "Community Fall Festival." In the vacant lots located next to Lee's Grocerteria and extending all the way into the downtown area, many new events were set up, including a turkey shoot, a largest pumpkin contest, rare fruit display, jellies, needlework, band concerts, motorcycle races and stunts, as well as music by the ukulele girls. Of particular note was a gentleman from Newport Mesa named Donald Dodge who exhibited two boxes of his prize-winning apples.

In 1918, the fair was once again held in Huntington Beach (October 1–5), in the same tents from the previous year. A local paper, the *Huntington Beach News*, referred to it as the "Second Annual Fall Fair." Based on how successful it had been the previous year, the 1918 version of the fair was expanded. It featured more than three hundred poultry coops, a huge array of floral products, rabbits, a library exhibit and large tractors and other farm equipment. An impressive replica of Orange County's harbor was displayed, and a parade was held to commemorate the fall fair that year. The Huntington Beach pier was decorated, and a huge party was thrown on the famed structure, replicating the celebration that had taken place when the new pier was unveiled four years earlier in 1914.

For all of the lack of specific information about the early years of the fair, Huntington Beach was lucky that city historian Jerry Person, in his much-read column in the *Huntington Beach Independent* newspaper, included a series of articles in 2006 that contained an impressive amount of detail on the years the fair was held in that city. Gleaned from original reporting in the old *Huntington Beach News*, Person wove together sparkling, detailed accounts that are presented here with permission. Crammed with interesting tidbits and facts, they are essential Orange County Fair artifacts from a very underreported era.

Over the many years our city of Huntington Beach has found many inventive ways to promote our town and its many events.

In many of these advertising stunts the automobile played an important part.

One of the earliest automobile parades advertising our town's event occurred on September 24, 1918 and this parade was formed to advertise our Second Annual Fall Fair that was to be held from Thursday, October 2nd to Sunday, October 5th of 1918.

To kick off the big event, Dr. R.H. Chapin organized a parade of cars that would travel into the various cities, towns, and hamlets in Orange County.

Each of these 15 cars would be decorated with banners, flags and bunting and would carry a delegation of prominent members of our community that would extol the virtues of the coming fair and our town.

This booster parade of cars left Huntington Beach at 9 a.m. with half of the cars going up the coast towards Seal Beach and this half was led by Dr. Chapin and the other half was led by Judge Louis Copeland and toured the communities of Wintersburg, Smeltzer and Westminster, with the two halves meeting up at Alamitos Road.

With all 15 cars together, the parade headed for Artesia and Norwalk in Los Angeles County before turning around and heading for Anaheim, Buena Park, Brea, Fullerton, La Habra, Placentia, Olive, Orange, Tustin, Santa Ana, Garden Grove and Talbert (Fountain Valley) before returning home.

Three Boy Scouts, Paul Adair, Earl Cochran and Gordon Talbert, went along with the delegation and handed out handbills to the public and window cards to the businesses along the way.

One of these cars included a pre-1915 brass-era car donated by the Union Rescue Mission in Santa Ana that carried Charles "Pop" Endicott who played an instrument called the Uniphone.

A brass car is one in which there was a lot of shiny brass trim on the radiator and headlights and this novel car was driven by Huntington Beach resident W.R. Anderson.

Another vehicle in the parade featured Mrs. H.A. Benning driving a big Hudson Super-six and carrying Mrs. H.L. Heffner, Mrs. H.V. Anderson and Mrs. A.C. Bullen.

These ladies were dressed as Red Cross nurses to represent the Huntington Beach branch of the American Red Cross.

As the parade of autos stopped in each town, Jesse Armitage and Alex Nelson, with megaphones in hand, spoke to the crowds that gathered about the cars.

Only one mishap occurred during this long parade, that being a flat tire to one of the cars as it traveled through Buena Park, but Charles Andrews quickly changed this.

Included in the parade delegation were Judge Charles Warner, Thomas Talbert, Maxine Farrar, Earl Farrar, James Conrad, Celia Bentley, Mary Turner, Mrs. Gale Bergey, Mary Starr, Margaret Lavering, Mary Jane Thatcher and her parents, Mary Van Fleet, Julia French, Irene Engle, Fern Irwin, Elizabeth Kerr, Minnie Steele, W.L. McKenney, F.H. McElfresh, T.R. Canady, J.K. McDonald, George Franklin, Henry Goestch, Daniel Huston, Charles Nutt, Pierce Tarbox and Lorraine Tarbox.

As you can see a great many of our townspeople contributed their time to the parade that advertised the fall fair.

This fair would be held at Main Street and Olive Avenue in our hometown of Huntington Beach and would be housed in three large tents and in a fourth already at the location that was being used for religious services.

Fair Committee Chairman George Franklin leased two 60x90 and one 60x120 foot tents for a cost of $175 and these three tents weighed over 3,000 pounds.

To save money, the fair committee secured poles for the tents from the Southern California Edison Co.

During this fair another parade would be held only this time it would feature a parade of young ladies attired in bathing suits.

This fall fair would become an important part of Huntington Beach history.

As plans progressed beyond all expectations, the idea came that this was more than a local community fair, but a larger county event and so on Wednesday night, September 18, 1918, the executive committee decided to change the name of the Second Annual Fall Fair to the Orange County Fair, a name we are all familiar with today.

Although there were small attempts at creating an Orange County Fair in the 1890s and into the 1900s, it was not until this fair in Huntington Beach that it truly became a countywide event.

We can thank the people of our town who help popularize this event in those 15 automobiles that traveled into every town and hamlet of our county advertising and promoting a truly Orange County event.

Next week we'll look at what transpired at this fair which I would like to call the birthplace of the Orange County Fair.

A HISTORY OF CELEBRATION

Two weeks ago we began looking back at Huntington Beach's 2nd Annual Fall Fair that would be held at Olive and Main and at various locations throughout our town from October 2 to October 5, 1918.

We learned of the grand parade of cars that toured many of our towns and cities in Orange and Los Angeles counties as a way to advertise this special event.

We also learned that just before the fair was to open, its name was changed from the Fall Fair to the Orange County Fair.

I believe that this event is very important in not only Huntington Beach history, but to the history of Orange County and to the history of the Orange County Fair that we celebrate today.

Even if there were older Orange County Fairs before this one, this one truly represented the county as a whole and would make Huntington Beach the birth place of this popular event.

Three weeks before the fair opened, the general committee chairman, F.H. McElfresh, to receive progress reports and suggestions, called a meeting of the various committees.

A letter was read from the manager of the Liberty Fair that would be held in Los Angeles a week after our fair closed and inviting a delegation from Huntington Beach come up and visit their fair.

They probably needed our expert input in putting on an event as successful as our Orange County Fair.

The committee members voted to accept their invitation and would send a local delegation to the Liberty Fair.

Floral Committee Chair Bertha Proctor reported that her committee is considering a Japanese tearoom at the fair with the proceeds going to the Red Cross.

Time was moving fast towards opening day and not all of the plans were still completed, but would there be enough time.

Two weeks before the start of the fair the committee chairs again met in the offices of our chamber of commerce to help finalize the events.

Willis Osborn from the Pacific Electric Railway reported that he felt sure that his company's band would be able to perform during the event.

A.J. Young, the Potato King, reported that most of the local ranchers would have some type of exhibit of their crops during the fair and that the ranchers were excited and honored to be part of this event.

Mary Newland of the canned fruits and jelly committee reported that because of the light crops and high prices there would be less fruit to be displayed.

General Committee Chairman McElfresh reported that a new committee had been added, a library committee, to be chaired by librarian Bertha Proctor.

This new committee would plan a display of war books, books on war conservation, Boy Scouts and children's books.

It was also reported that on the last day of the fair, a bathing beauty parade would be held with some of the cutest O.C. girls you ever saw.

With time getting closer to the big day, another committee meeting was called for last minute items and reports.

H.T. Dunning reported that there would be about 300 exhibits of poultry, about 30 goats and some pigs and that a trough would be needed to feed the hogs.

It was arranged that a 30-piece Military Band from Fort McArthur would play for the first and third days of the fair and the Naval Reserve Band of 56 members would entertain the public on the second day.

A bandstand would be erected at Main Street and Walnut Avenue and seats for the public would be placed on Walnut so the visitors could rest and listen to the music.

A state picnic would be held on the last day of the fair.

Picnic Chair Bertha Proctor read a letter from C.H. Parsons, secretary of the affiliated state societies of Southern California, stating that he and their president would be visiting our fair.

Proctor reported that there was no money available for banners or badges, but that she would paint some cards with state flowers to be placed on the various state tables.

R.E. Lee was appointed chairman of the Arkansas picnic and City Marshal John Tinsley of the Texas picnic.

Mrs. T.W. Cadd would chair the Native California picnic and Elizabeth Kerr, Fred Day and George Bentley would team up to head the Canadian picnic.

Other states to be included were Minnesota, Wisconsin, Illinois, Kansas, Nebraska, Iowa, Indiana, Missouri, Colorado, New York, Pennsylvania, Ohio, Wyoming, Montana and New England.

Our town would be pulling out all the stops to make this a truly historic event and one that they hoped would bring praise to Huntington Beach and its people.

Don't think our local schools would be left out of such an important event, oh no, a huge parade of youngsters from Huntington Beach, Ocean View, Seal Beach, Westminster, Bolsa, Fountain Valley, Newport Beach and Harper would parade through town on the second day of the fair.

Barker Brothers furniture store from Los Angeles would be having a display of electrical appliances for the lady of the house.

To be displayed would be sewing machines, washing machines, vacuum cleaners and fireless cookers, all powered by electricity.

Barker Brothers would also be serving biscuits, hot ham and coffee to their visitors with the profits going to the Red Cross war effort and they would be serving dinner free of charge to the members of the military bands.

R.C. Turner of the music committee arranged to have on hand Amon Dorsey Caine and Ethel Smith as part of the fair's entertainment.

Even the Princess Theatre got into the spirit and would be showing Pershing's Crusaders, *a government war movie, on the last two days of the fair.*

Remember that World War I was still being fought and that the patriotic spirit was strong here in Huntington Beach and for many this fair was a way to forget the war for just a little while.

Next week we'll conclude our look at Huntington Beach's Orange County Fair, its people and events that made it so memorable.

This week we'll continue our look back at what could possibly be considered the birthplace of our Orange County Fair of today.

As we learned there were earlier Orange County Fairs, but these were mainly small local affairs, whereas this one would encompass nearly the whole of Orange County.

This event had started out as the Second Annual Fall Fair that was to be held at the corner of Main Street and Olive Avenue from October 2nd to the 5th of 1918.

But as the displays grew in number the fair committee on September 18, 1918 officially renamed the event the Orange County Fair.

This event had grown so large, well beyond all expectations, that it had now had the makings of a true countywide event rather than just a local affair.

The fair would be held in four large tents and at several locations around town.

As the big day approached, excitement stirred our citizens and committees finalized their displays, events and programs.

J.A. Armitage and Gladyse Bollon of the singing committee went searching for the music of "Over There" and "There's a Long, Long

Trail" for use by the singers in the community singing program at the pavilion.

The greatest celebration and fair in Orange County's history began on Wednesday, October 4th with a salute to Liberty and Newport Mesa Day.

The big war tank "Liberty" came into town and caused many a head to turn as it rolled along Main Street to its final stop at Main and 17th Street.

A large delegation of our city officials and private citizens met the tank as it pulled beside the bandstand.

The tank was there to help sell the public liberty bonds and Albert Onson of Huntington Beach Sheet Metal Works was the first to step up and purchase a bond in the name of his two-year-old son, John Albert Onson.

The second bond sold that day went to Huntington Beach furniture storeowner, Carl Olson.

Throughout the day patriotic citizens stepped up to buy liberty bonds, much as our citizens would do after the Second World War.

During that first day $41,200 worth of bonds were sold.

Accompanying the tank were vaudeville actress Kathleen Clifford, James Hogan and J.H. Galart of Los Angeles and J. Lowenstein of Valparaiso, Indiana.

Those purchasing bonds that first day could have them autographed by Clifford while Huntington Beach City Attorney Alex P. Nelson and the city attorney from Orange spoke to the attendees.

Inside the main tent would be found some of the finest exhibits of farm products ever to be seen in Southern California.

A delegation from the town of Downey sent twenty-five of its citizens, headed by Downey's Community Fair President, W.M. Booth, to inspect our event.

Inside the Biggs building on Main Street the ladies of Orange County offered a huge display of fancy needlework to the delight of the fairgoers.

A display of Fordson, Lambert, Trundaar, Bear Cat and Los Angeles Auto Tractors attracted a good many of our local farmers who marveled at what these machines could do.

In another tent Joseph Vavra of the Huntington Beach Nursery had a magnificent display of over 225 varieties of dahlias in bloom.

Another interesting sight at the fair was the goat exhibit along with exhibits of hogs, rabbits and poultry.

Inside a tent erected next to the Princess Theatre on Main Street a display of Junior Red Cross items was given by our local grammar school children.

Music for the first day was furnished by the military band from Fort McArthur and Bertha Proctor's library exhibit was an added feature to this year's fair and a popular one too.

The next day was a salute to War Savings and Peatland Day and was to have begun with a parade of our county's school children, but rain that morning postponed the parade until the afternoon.

This parade was headed by Harold Campbell who was dressed as a sailor and followed by children dressed to represent the United States and its Allies of World War I.

The Newport Beach Chamber of Commerce brought in a replica of Orange County's harbor on the second day of the fair.

This featured small boats sailing about the harbor and was of great interest to both old and young.

Because of the rain that morning, the community singers were moved into the Princess Theatre from the pavilion where a program of singing was given including guest singers Ethel Smith and Amon Cain of Los Angeles.

Music for this program was furnished by the Naval Reserve Band of San Pedro and was a welcome treat from the rain.

The Barker Brothers exhibit of fireless cookers, sewing machines, vacuum cleaners and other household appliances run by electricity were a great hit by the ladies of our county.

At this exhibit Eva Scott of Los Angeles and her ladies prepared and served countless ham sandwiches and hot coffee to the attendees with the proceeds going to the Red Cross.

One of the unusual exhibits at the fair was a German helmet on display at the Information tent that came from Remi Nadeau of the Rainbow division in France and this was sent to the fair by mail with a 12-cent stamp attached.

Next week we'll wind-up our look at the last two days of this historic event that would later become one of our county's biggest and best beloved events.

For the last few weeks we have been looking at the birth of the Orange County Fair that was held in our own Huntington Beach in 1918 and this

week we'll conclude our look back at the people and the events that made it so memorable so many years ago.

We learned in those weeks that this fair began as Huntington Beach's 2nd Annual Fall Fair, but with the tremendous turnout of exhibitors from Orange County, the fair committee decided to rename this event, the Orange County Fair.

This historic event would run for four whole days, from October 2nd to the 5th and would involve so many of our residents in this event.

The fair would be held in four huge tents erected at the corner of Main Street and Olive Avenue and also at several smaller locations around town.

This week we'll look at the last two days of this great event and at some of the people who were involved in making it so successful.

This fair came at a time when so many of our county's men were fighting the Kaiser's troops overseas during World War I and this event gave many in Orange County an opportunity to escape from the war at home and the memories of their sons abroad.

On the third day of the fair the Naval Band entertained the public with a concert as Liberty Loan Day and Orange County Day was celebrated.

To help in making this event a success, many of our local businesses donated cash or prizes.

By today's standards these prizes may seem trivial, but you must remember that this was a time when a dollar was worth a dollar.

To prove the point the Beach Broom Co. donated a broom worth a dollar for the best group of tatting by one individual and Sarrabere Cleaners donated a dollar to the person catching the greased pig.

The Kandy Kitchen donated a five-pound box of candy as a first prize to the winner of the bathing suit contest and Dalany's Fruit Store's donation was a 25-pound basket of fruit to the winner of the boys and girls tug-of-war contest.

B.S. White offered a box of cigars to the winner of the baseball game and B.T. Mollica donated a pair of ladies tennis shoes to the winner of the women's swimming race.

One of the chief attractions at the fair was the agricultural exhibit held inside the main tent.

A.J. Young had an exhibit of a liberty ship filled with the finest potatoes one could imagine that were grown on his ranch just north of town.

Donald Dodge from the town of Harper on the Newport Mesa had a giant display of various varieties of apples that were better than any outside the Garden of Eden.

He had brought from his ranch boxes of Delicious, Winter Banana, Winter Pearmain and Yellow Bellflower apples from his four year old trees.

As the public entered this tent, the first display to be seen was a huge display of produce grown on the farm in the Fairview section of the Newport Mesa by George Hall.

Besides the events in the tents that third day there was held at the beach an airplane exhibition of flying skill as the plane flew along our beach before it landed and the crowd was able to inspect the plane firsthand.

The last day was celebrated as Red Cross Day and Home Coming Day with many state picnics taking place on our beach along with a bathing suit parade, a street carnival and dancing throughout the night.

Many of our local companies had displays in this historic fair.

The La Bolsa Tile Co. had one of the largest exhibits of tiles and the Pacific Oilcloth & Linoleum Co. used the fair to introduce its new product "Fibrola," a cloth made from paper as a substitute for oilcloth.

The Beach Broom Co. featured a large display of locally made brooms, the Arrow Garage had on display the new Hupmobile automobile and the E.L. Pearce Cannery had an exhibit of its solid packed tomatoes.

An interesting amusement attraction for the public was the "goat chute" originated by Harold Campbell, the principal of our grammar school, in which balls are thrown at a small hole in a canvas.

When a ball went through the hole, a lever was struck and released a platform that allowed a kid goat to come sliding down a chute.

About 20 lovely ladies took part in the bathing suit parade and the winner of that box of candy donated by the Kandy Kitchen went to Mrs. R.H. Chapin.

Also taking part in the bathing suit contest was H.V. Anderson, cashier at the Huntington Beach Company office, who was dressed up in a regulation "cop" uniform and chased a clown around as the girls paraded about the stage.

Local real estate man C.D. Heartwell provided a display of three generations of razors from his family and Reverend C. Carey Willett of the Baptist church displayed a collection of antique books that dated back to 1538.

There were so many prizes awarded at the fair to our residents and one of these went to Minnie Higgins who won first prize for her dried corn.

Others winning first prizes included H.A. Gallienne for his parsnips, William Newland for his British Queen potatoes and Mabel Anderson for her oil paintings.

As the people danced the night away, the tents closed its displays and the fair ended.

A week after the fair closed a meeting was held at the library attended by the various committees to discuss how the fair went and what could be done to make next year's event even better.

During this meeting Mrs. W.E. Gerhart suggested that a room be provided for the members of the bands, who this year had no place to go during the rainstorm and the committees all agreed to that suggestion.

H.L. Heffner believed it was time to organize a true County Fair and made a motion that an Orange County Fair Association be formed and this was seconded by Huntington Beach Trustee E.E. French.

From this humble beginning in 1918, the Orange County Fair has grown into a huge event, and Huntington Beach and its citizens were an important part in its rich history.

With the war going badly and many of our Huntington Beach boys fighting in the military, morale at the home front needed a boost.

The burdens of our townspeople were being stretched to their limits.

What with nightly blackouts, air raid drills and the threat of a surprise attack on our oil fields, it was no wonder our residents needed an outlet for their emotions.

Going to church helped, but with the town's Fourth of July parade canceled, our people needed some kind of community involvement to take their minds off the war.

This came about in a round about way when the Huntington Beach Garden Club began to plan their small fall festival event for their members in 1943.

But as their ideas grew, so did the size of the event.

With the help of Bill Gallienne and several local townspeople the Garden Club's fall festival began to evolve into an old time three day Country Fair.

There would be bands, prizes, carnival rides, a carnival midway and famous people appearing.

Main Street would be decorated with corn stalks, pumpkins and an old fashioned husking bee.

Old surreys and hay wagons would be parked at street corners to give the business area a country look.

The Pav-a-lon would be converted into a country "corn palace" with banners and beautiful senoritas playing guitars, singing and dancing to early California tunes.

The idea was suggested that local merchants and residents dress in country attire and when this was presented to the people everyone liked the idea.

Eve Druxman and Jack Robertson were in charge of the costuming.

As plans were being made, more and more of our residents began to take part in the event that would be held on September 14, 15, & 16, 1943.

Nearly half the town volunteered to be on some committee and there were well over 35 committees, from Farmers Committee to Canned Fruits & Vegetable Committees to Cacti Committee, Flower Committee. Well you get the idea there were a lot of committees.

Bill Gallienne of the H.B. Chamber of Commerce prepared a 36 page booklet explaining the how and what you can enter into the fair.

He mailed 2,000 of these booklets to the housewives living in the Huntington Beach area.

Even our city council got into the spirit of a country fair by letting the fair be held in front of the pier and the use of the Pav-a-lon.

The area in front of the pier would be turned into a carnival midway complete with a Ferris wheel, merry-go-round and other midway attractions.

Huntington Beach Mayor Tom Talbert authorized the use of city equipment and police and firemen during the three day event.

Now what would a country fair be without a "Fair Queen" and this fair would have one, only this queen would be chosen a little differently.

She would be chosen by which girl sold the most war bonds up to the day before the fair began and that girl would reign as fair queen.

Seven local girls entered the contest and these girls were Mary Louise Chamness, Florence Dale, Lee Dodge, Colleen Gotschalk, Hildreth Clark, Florence Pederson and Eileen Riley.

By now the fears of war were pushed to the back of the mind as everyone started pitching in to make this event a big success.

The reception committee invited personal from several Army & Navy bases to the event.

Included were Colonel Bennie Bierman, Colonel Dick Hanley, Captain Clipper Smith, Captain Marcus M. McCallen, Major Sam Houston Flanagan, Ensign John Hawley and baseball legend Sgt. Joe DiMaggio.

At 8:00 p.m. on the evening before the opening of the fair, War Bond Chairman George J. Wheat announced that Hildreth Clark had sold the highest dollar amount of war bonds and would be crowned queen in the ballroom of the Pav-a-lon on opening day.

The doors of the Pav-a-lon were opened wide at 6:00 p.m. to admit over 2500 people who came to watch as Colonel Dick Hanley of the Marines crowned Hildreth Clark "Queen of the Huntington Beach Country Fair."

Music for the first day was provided by the Long Beach Women's Symphony, the U.S. Navy Coast Guard Band and the Huntington Beach Girls' Chorus under the direction of Dr. Ralph Hawes.

On the second day of the fair the doors were opened at 1:00 p.m. and the day was known as "Long Beach Day" and at 2:00 p.m. a baby show was given.

People came from all over to ride the Ferris wheel and partake of the midway treats.

The Main Street merchants got dressed up in their best country clothes.

That evening the Long Beach Municipal Band played along with entertainment by the Vera Downs singers.

The many committees now spent many long hours judging all those entries of jams, jellies, hobbies, baked goods, flowers, etc. that make up a real old time country fair and award the ribbons to the best.

On the last day of the fair was "Road to Romance" Day and there was a livestock show at the corner of Main Street and Orange Avenue.

At noon the Old Settlers Picnic was held with Bill Gallienne showing up in a ten gallon hat, red flannel shirt, cut away coat, cowboy boots and a big red dahlia in his buttonhole.

George Wardwell wore a full evening attire complete with a high top silk hat and cane.

After the picnic a Milkmaid's milking contest was held and after that came a parade of livestock down Main Street and after that came a dog show.

The 140th Infantry Band gave a concert in the evening at the Pav-a-lon.

Mayor Talbert called Bill Gallienne up on stage and Gallienne told the audience of the first Country Fair started in Huntington Beach in about 1915.

Louise Jenkins of the Garden Club was thanked for her untiring efforts at making this event so successful.

And for those three wonderful days and the weeks that preceded it, the fair brought a measure of joy and relief that lifted the burdens of war from the hearts of every Huntington Beach resident that year.

Last week we read of how the simple idea of a fall festival by the Huntington Beach Garden Club grew into a three-day Country Fair.

This was so successful that the garden club decided to stage a second Country Fair in 1944 and who better to lead and plan this event then Bill Gallienne.

Beginning in March of 1944, Gallienne assembled the people for the various committees.

Aiding Gallienne in this endeavor were members of the fair's Executive Committee composed of Gallienne, Huntington Beach Mayor Tom Talbert, last years Garden Club president Louise Jenkins, Mona Nevins, Harold Hepburn and Nancy Pann.

Like last year, the fair would be sponsored by the Huntington Beach Garden Club and this year Reginald "Scotty" Hudson held the position of president of that organization.

One of the first issues for the executive committee to face was the fair's theme and the committee came up with "California Under Twelve Flags."

There would be twelve flags displayed during the four-day event.

Money would be needed and that was the responsibility of the Finance Committee composed of Jessie Mauldin, Wayne Pickering, David Todd, Charles Burleycamp, Fred Mauldin and Grace Scott.

As in the previous year the city did not have a Fourth of July parade in 1944 either, so this event would serve as a replacement for our famous July event.

One new event at the Country Fair would be the addition of a Southern California Twins contest and who would have known that this event would become a major event in future years.

What would a country fair be without its beauty contest and like the 1943 fair, this one would have its beauty contest too.

Wherein last year the young lady who sold the most war bonds was chosen queen of the fair, this year it would be the girl who sold the most season tickets for the fair between August 1st to August 15th.

The girls would be under the watchful eye of Eve Druxman, who chaired the Queen and Coronation Committee.

The fair itself would begin on Thursday, August 17 and run to Sunday, August 20.

Thirteen girls entered the contest to be queen of the fair: Jeanette Adair, Corynne Bose, Catherine Case, Grace Cerda, Patricia Coe, Dorothy

Harper, Bertha Henslick, Ida Kratz, Barbara Lee, Virginia Nichols, Barbara Whitfield, Beth Wise and Virginia Wise.

On the last day of the contest Druxman announced that 19-year-old Grace Cerda had sold the most season tickets and would be the queen.

Mona Nevins and her ticket and gate committee met for one last time and were now ready to handle the large crowds in a quick and efficient manner.

As the big day arrived, the Main Street merchants would again don their best country costumes.

Bill Gallienne donned his "Diamond Jim" Brady outfit while members of the Woman's Club dressed in their best old fashioned dresses.

The fair began with a parade down Main Street to the beach and included music by the Long Beach Municipal Band, groups of WACs, WAVEs, the fair queen and her court and, of course, the Fair Committee members.

There were displays of all manner of homemade goods, baked, grown, sewed or canned.

The Southern California Water Co. had a display that showed how much water was lost by a dripping faucet.

The American Legion's booth had a display of guns that were in use before the war.

The Huntington Beach Lions Club took up a collection and bought 12 trophies to be given out as "First Prizes."

The Woman's Club's exhibit included a depiction of the front of the White House with Miss Stars and Stripes and Miss Liberty standing in front.

There would be a baby show and revue, a Dahlia and Begonia show.

Main Street was roped off for a horse parade and show.

In Lake Park a barbecue was given by the Native Songs of the Golden West.

H.L. Hillman won a "First Prize" for his rabbit and Myrtle Harman won the fastest milking contest.

These are just a few of the many activities in the fair of 1944 and of how our residents banded together to put on a city wide event during those dark days of World War II.

I mentioned the casualties of war, well even these can be a blessing as when Uncle Sam needed the land in Seal Beach where the old Sam's Seafood stood (2501 Coast Highway) for their weapons depot.

This forced the restaurant to relocate where it is today on PCH and they even brought with them their famous Sword Fish landmark for the new location and it sits today on the roof in their new and bigger location.

Vivid, telling and detailed, these articles remain some of the most factual and colorful accounts of the early days of the Orange County Fair. The next three years, through 1920, the fair continued to be held in Huntington Beach. As you have read, the fair made a profound impact on the beach community. But it was time to move on.

Chapter 2

THE 1920s

In 1921, the Santa Ana Chamber of Commerce assumed fair sponsorship for temporary grounds that were built on East Fruit Street and Grand Avenue in Santa Ana, near the train depot. The fair this year ran from September 28 through October 1. Departments included citrus, beekeepers, poultry, home demonstrations, high-producing dairy cows and purebred bulls. This was the first year the dairy livestock were featured at the Orange County Fair and also the first year that the Valencia Orange Show was held in nearby Anaheim.

The California Valencia Orange Show had been started by the Anaheim Chamber of Commerce to showcase the region's most vital product. At the very first show in May 1921, there was a telephone address given to the people by President Warren G Harding, whose sister hailed from Santa Ana.

In July 1922, the Huntington Beach Chamber of Commerce asked the Farm Bureau to take over management of the Orange County Fair. The Farm Bureau offered Santa Ana Chamber of Commerce to participate, and the joint committee located the fair closer to the train depot. Additionally, the fair now included exhibits with automobiles.

Here's an interesting news item from the *Pacific Rural Press* in August 1922:

> *The Orange County Fair, which has been held at Huntington Beach for the past five years, will be greatly enlarged and held at the central point of the county, Santa Ana, September 27–30. At least ten Farm Centers will compete in the community agricultural displays, and provision is*

A rare Orange County Fair scrapbook from 1922. *Courtesy Orange County Fair archives.*

now made for a real exhibit of the fine livestock produced in Orange and nearby counties. About 90,000 square feet will be under canvas. The Fair Committee, headed by D. Eyman Huff, has engaged J.C. Metzgar of Santa Ana as secretary-manager.

Also that year, carrier pigeons carried Orange County Fair news to Fullerton newspapers. A four-legged chicken was also exhibited at the 1922 fair.

Another popular fair in the region, the Los Angeles County Fair, was created in 1922. Taking place in October in a former beet field in Pomona, California, highlights of this inaugural event included harness racing, chariot races and an airplane wing walking exhibition. The Los Angeles County Fair would go on to become one of the largest county fairs the United States and today is the fourth largest in the country.

The fair remained in Santa Ana in 1923, taking place from September 25 to September 29. Now run by the Orange County Farm Bureau, attendance records were shattered as forty thousand spectators came out to experience the fair. Gate receipts were sufficient to meet all costs and actually secure $5,000 worth of property for future use.

The 1924 edition of the Orange County Fair was scheduled to take place from September 23 to September 27. But the fair wound up being canceled due to a foot-and-mouth epidemic. Just how serious was this crisis? The following was an amendment issued by the Department of Agriculture:

Amendment 1 to B.A.I. Order 336—To Spread of Foot-and-Mouth Disease I Sheep, Other Ruminants, and Swine (Effective on and after May 4, 1932) TTLE, United States Department of Agriculture, Office of the Secretary, Washington, D.C, May 4, 19S2.

The fact has been determined by the Secretary of Agriculture, and notice is hereby given, that a contagious and communicable disease, known as foot-and-mouth disease, exists in livestock in the State of California in an area not covered by the quarantine established by B.A.I. Order 336, dated April 29, 1932, and effective on April 29, 1932. Now, therefore, I, Arthur M. Hyde, Secretary of Agriculture, under authority conferred by section 1 of the act of Congress approved March 3, 1905 (33 Stat. 1264), do hereby quarantine all that portion of Los Angeles County, Calif., lying within the following boundary lines: Beginning at the inter-section of Somerset and South Streets in the city of Long Beach, thence running east on South Street and continuing east on First Street to Main Street, thence running south on Main Street and Dohn Avenue to the Orange County line, thence running southwest on the Orange County line to Spring Street, thence running west on Spring Street to Somerset Street, thence running north on Somerset Street to the point of beginning, and do hereby amend said B.A.I. Order 336 by extending as herein provided the quarantined area established in said-mentioned order. It is further ordered by this amendment 1 to B.A.I. Order 336, under the authority and discretion conferred on the Secretary of Agriculture by section 3 of the act of Congress approved March 3, 1905 (33 Stat. 1264), and section 2 of the act of Congress approved February 2, 1903 (32 Stat. 791), that the interstate or foreign movement of cattle, sheep, other ruminants, and swine, from, into, or through said quarantined area, and the interstate or foreign shipments of the dressed carcasses of calves, sheep, and other ruminants, and of the hides, skins, and hoofs of cattle, sheep, and other ruminants, and of all hay, straw, or similar fodder from any point in the said-mentioned quarantined area shall be made only in accordance with and subject in all respects to the conditions, requirements, and restrictions of said B.A.I. Order 336. This amendment which for the purpose of identification is designated as amendment 1 to B.A.I. Order 336, shall become and be effective on and after May 4, 1932. Done at Washington this 4th day of May, 1932. Witness my hand and the seal of the Department of Agriculture. Arthur M. Hyde, Secretary of Agriculture.

Even though there was no fair, some local poultry men still exhibited at the fair in Pomona and won honors. Orange County orange growers exhibited at the National Orange Show in San Bernardino.

In 1925, the fair took place from September 22 to September 26 at a new set of fairgrounds located across the highway from Orange County Hospital in Santa Ana. This was the year the first Orange County Fair board was elected. The fair, sponsored by the Farm Bureau, was one of the best held from an agricultural standpoint. The main agricultural tent was taken up by community features and educational exhibits. Industrial, poultry, dog and livestock tents; amusement at Midway; rodeo each afternoon; allegorical stories each evening depicting the development of Orange County; and more locally based events all proved to be true crowd pleasers.

One year later, the fair was moved again, to a location on State College Boulevard on the border of what is now the city of Orange. The fair was also expanded to six days, from September 6 to September 11, and hailed as the "10th Annual Orange County Fair." Attempts were also made at this

Left: A program from the 1928 Orange County Fair. *Courtesy Orange County Fair archives.*

Below: A 1929 Cretors popcorn wagon at the Orange County fairgrounds on October 18, 1950. This wagon was later displayed at the Briggs Cunningham Automotive Museum. *Courtesy Orange County Archives.*

point in time to obtain a permanent fairground for housing the fair and also to house the Valencia Orange Show. To that end, fair officials purchased seventeen acres of the Orange Grove district.

In 1927, the fair took on an official theme for the first time: "Old-Time County Fair." Seven tents in all were erected, with an "Indian motif" predominating in many tents. Supervisors of six California counties were guests, the Huntington Beach Municipal Band was on hand to play concerts and the famous Riders of the West took part in fair rodeo contests. At this point, another twenty-two acres were purchased adjoining the original seventeen in an attempt to expand the fairgrounds at a permanent site.

The 1928 fair, held from September 3 to September 9, presented even bigger and better attractions, but bad weather held back the crowds. The Agricultural Extension Service of University of California was credited for the great success of three major divisions: rare and subtropical fruit, small grant and the Junior Fair.

The 1929 fair, held from August 28 to September 2, was themed "Pioneer Day," and one of the most prominent attractions was an Indian village. C.C. Chapman opened the ceremonies, and tent shows included concerts, rodeos and many exhibits. More than $17,000 in prizes were awarded.

Chapter 3

THE 1930s

The first fair of the new decade, held from September 30 to October 5, was themed "The League of Nations." Each exhibit was awarded extra points for using the theme. The League of Nations, of course, was an international organization created to promote world peace and cooperation that was created by the Treaty of Versailles in 1919—it would last until 1946. In 1930, the Orange County Fair included farm exhibits, floriculture, livestock, poultry, rabbits, basket displays, domestic art, needlework, baking, canning, roping, riding and jumping.

The 1931 fair, held from June 4 to June 14, was special in that it was combined with the Valencia Orange Show into one giant event called the Orange County Valencia Orange Show and Fair. The theme was "The Golden Days of Montezuma," and the fair featured three great entertaining and educationally themed features: twelve citrus displays, twelve agricultural features and a mammoth industrial display. The fifth annual packing contest, a model packing plant in action, fine arts, culinary and domestic exhibits, as well as the "Joy Zone" carnival, were also enjoyed by thousands of patrons that summer.

From 1932 to 1938, the Orange County Fair participated in a huge Tri-County Fair comprising Los Angeles, Riverside and Orange Counties. Throughout those years, although conjoined with two other events, the Orange County Fair still managed to distinguish itself within the larger event and introduced an even greater variety of attractions. In 1933, a premier horseracing program and night horse show were added. In 1934,

An image from the 1930 fair, held near the border of Anaheim and Orange on State College Boulevard. *Courtesy Orange County Fair archives.*

A 1931 invite to the then president of Mexico, Pascual Ortiz Rubio (he did not attend). *Courtesy Orange County Fair archives.*

under the theme of "Most Beautiful in America," the sixteen-day event from September 15 to September 30 took in thirty thousand entries vying for $100,000 in prizes. The event, held in Pomona, featured horse racing every afternoon and myriad new livestock and agricultural attractions. Cornelia Beversluis, seventeen, from Norwalk was the winner of the 1934 "Farmerette" championship.

BACK IN POMONA IN 1935, thirty thousand entries once again competed, this time for $125,000 in prize money. About $50,000 in purses was given out during seventeen days and three nights of fun-filled action. About $20,000 went to the livestock division; $6,000 went to small stock poultry, rabbits and pigeons; and $2,000 went to the women's department for best pies, cakes, canned goods and needlework. County fairs were becoming some of the most popular events throughout Southern California, thanks in large part to this wonderful event that continued to feature three separate counties. Of course, the competitions featuring cash prizes were a huge draw for people.

The 1936 event at the Pomona Fairgrounds featured thirty thousand varied exhibits, and the daily horse racing made the event even more popular than ever. On Sunday, September 20, a "Greatest Historical Parade" was held as a procession of "Golden Memories" recounted the romantic story of California; gorgeous floats and picturesque groups entered by communities throughout the Southland dazzled the attendees. One thousand costumed people and five hundred horses participated in this unforgettable event.

The fair just continued to grow bigger and better. In 1938, the final year of the huge Tri-County fair, more than $1 million in improvements were added to the event. There were now fifty exhibit buildings, $150,000 in cash prizes, more horse racing and some of the most spectacular horse shows audiences had ever seen up to that point. Glen Gray and his celebrated Casa Loma Orchestra were featured performers at the fair that year, and four "All-American" contests were introduced: the National Percheron show, the National Sculpture competition, the National Amaryllis show and the National Croquet Match.

From 1939 to 1941, the fair was held back in Santa Ana at the Municipal Bowl, a stadium on Civic Center Drive that a few years later, in 1945, would be the site of Ronald Reagan's first political speech. The first year it was moved here, the fair was officially rebranded as the "Orange County Fair and Horse Show," and the Assistance League of Santa Ana voted to make an application of $6,000 to cover the premium list from state funds. Any profits from the fair would benefit the Children's Hospital

A bee display by Yorba Linda's "Clover Leaf" 4-H Club, circa 1940s. *Courtesy Orange County Archives.*

fund. Ed Stinson and Harry Odgen of Pomona entered with six horse hitches. The California Fruit Growers Exchange donated full equipment for the production of fresh orange juice, with the proceeds going toward the maintenance of charity beds at the St. Joseph and Santa Ana Valley Hospitals. There was a huge parade held on Saturday at noon starting at the Santa Ana Municipal Bowl. A small start for an Orange County Fair was made in June of this year when the Santa Ana assistance league, which had been having an annual horse show for the past few years, invited farm centers and 4-H clubs to enter exhibits for which cash prizes were offered. The exhibits were well received, and cash awards totaling about $500 were given to the clubs and members participating.

The introduction of the 4-H clubs would become a vital and integral part of the fair for years to come. 4-H is a youth organization administered by the National Institute of Food and Agriculture of the United States Department of Agriculture. Its mission, first noted around 1902, was to "engage youth to reach their fullest potential while advancing the field of

Orange County Fair, August 1949. *Courtesy Orange County Archives.*

Orange County fairgrounds, June 26, 1949. *Courtesy Orange County Archives.*

youth development." The name 4-H represents four personal development areas of focus for the organization: head, heart, hands and health. The 4-H motto is "To make the best better," and its official slogan is "Learn by doing."

Since the focal point of 4-H has always been an idea of practical and hands-on learning for young people, it helped bridge the gap between public school education and rural life. To this day, 4-H plays a huge part in the Orange County Fair, as well as other fairs around the country.

Chapter 4

THE 1940s

For the first fair of the new decade, which was held from June 7 to June 9, 4-H club members participated in exhibits and events to a greater extent than the year before. Youth were finding their foothold at the fair, not just from 4-H but also from the Future Farmers of America (FFA), another youth program designed to foster an appreciation of agriculture among young people, founded in 1928. Additionally, the Orange County Fair and Horse Show attracted entries from nine different clubs, which entered nine different exhibits. There were twenty-one calves, sheep and swine featured at the show in addition to eggs, honey and vegetables. More than $400 was awarded in premiums to 4-H clubs and members. Sponsored by the Assistance League of Orange County, the fair was held again at the Santa Ana Municipal Bowl. Movie actor Jack Seal and the horse Weedpatch were two features at the fair that year. Mrs. A.J. Smith took home the blue ribbon with her prize-winning Shetland pony, Lady Helen. Also, bananas grown at nearby Santa Ana High School were exhibited at the fair.

In 1941, the fair dates ran from June 6 to June 8. Once again sponsored by Assistance League of Orange County, this year's fair featured Leo Carillo, the popular motion picture star and political cartoonist. Mrs. A.J. Smith was once again a feature at the fair with her Hackney ponies, and the Sonny Moore mule act also performed. And once again, local 4-H clubs played prominent parts at the fair. Ten clubs entered feature booths. Among the livestock entered by 4-H members were fifteen beef and ten dairy calves and seventeen head of sheep and pigs. About $450

Willis Warner crowns Betty Trichler, Orange County Fair Queen, 1949. *Courtesy Orange County Archives.*

Janet Gurney of Garden Grove Orange County Fair Queen candidate, with corsair fighter, August 1949. *Courtesy Orange County Archives.*

Flag raising at the Orange County Fair, July 19, 1949. *Courtesy Orange County Archives.*

Opposite, top: Orange County Fair exhibit, circa 1940s. *Courtesy Orange County Archives.*

Opposite, bottom: Orange County Fair plans, July 15, 1949. *Courtesy Orange County Fair archives.*

was awarded in prize money to club members. The fair this year was held back in Anaheim near La Palma Stadium in conjunction with the Anaheim's Festival and Parade.

Between the years of 1942 and 1947, there were no fairs due to World War II. Federal government mandates prevented large county fairs to help conserve war-related products such as petroleum, rubber and so on. However, local groups continued to hold small community parades, picnics and Fourth of July celebrations where crops and livestock were displayed. While exact locations are not known today, there were continued fair-like celebrations at small community gatherings throughout Orange County.

The fair returned in 1948 and was held once more in Anaheim, October 28–31. The theme was "Kiddieland," and the event was also presented as part of the Anaheim Halloween Parade. Concessions for food and skill games were sponsored by churches, the chamber of commerce, the American Legion and more. There was a special Orange County birthday cake exhibit and a quarter mile of booths and stalls with

Orange County Fair, August 1949. *Courtesy Orange County Archives.*

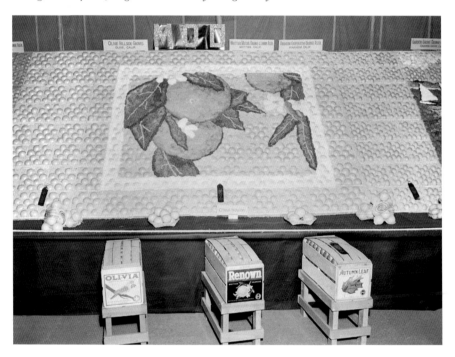

Mutual Orange Distributors (MOD) citrus display, Orange County Fair, 1949. *Courtesy Orange County Fair archives.*

the carnival, which included a double Ferris wheel and even a wildlife show. Orange County historian Chris Jepsen noted on his O.C. History Roundup blog:

The last pre–Costa Mesa fair was held in Anaheim in October 1948, to coincide with the twenty-fifth anniversary of Anaheim's traditional Halloween parade and celebration. The fair ran only four days. The theme for the 1948 fair was youth. There was lots of 4-H activity and involvement by 12 local high schools. Miss Phyllis Applegate of Huntington Beach High School was named queen of the fair and greeted Governor Earl Warren at an official reception. The 1948 Fair also featured all the usual country fair standbys, like baked goods, garden and agricultural products, and displays from all the local chambers of commerce.

For all the moving around the Orange County Fair had done up until this point, that was all about to stop. It was about to find a permanent home.

Following World War II, the Thirty-second District Agricultural Association was formed by the state of California, and it took on the task of running the fair. The state purchased land from the Santa Ana Army Air Base and set some of it aside for use as a new fairgrounds. In 1949, the fair became a five-day-long event and was relocated to the old army base, which quickly became the permanent location.

A 4-H event, Orange County Fair, August 1949. *Courtesy Orange County Archives.*

Orange County Fair Administration Building, 1949. *Courtesy Orange County Archives.*

Orange County Fair buildings, October 1952. *Courtesy Orange County Archives.*

There was much excitement over the new facility. On August 17, the day before the fair officially opened, the *Los Angeles Times* reported:

> *An old-time country fair in the unusual setting of a converted army base will attract thousands of visitors to the Orange County Fair*

Fair manager Bob Fullenwider and Dan Patch (of the Patch & Curtis Advertising Agency) at the Orange County Fair, 1949. *Courtesy Orange County Archives.*

which opens tomorrow. Farm products and community displays will be on exhibition for a four-day showing through Sunday at the new permanent Fairgrounds 6 miles south of here in Newport Boulevard the 32nd agricultural District Association has adapted a variety of former Army base buildings and added three large tents to house the many exhibits and farm products. Emphasis has been placed on home county entertainment features. Gates open at 10 AM tomorrow with dedication ceremonies including acceptance of the deed to the fairgrounds by H Clay Kellogg, president. The fair is using about 50 acres of the 175 acre tract, providing huge parking areas and former paved parade grounds. All servicemen who trained at the base are being welcomed free, by merely writing to the fair with details of their service. The four-day horse show will be presented in a big new arena tomorrow, Friday and Saturday evenings and Sunday afternoon. A top ranking vaudeville show will close at the fair Sunday evening.

Orange County Fair ribbon cutting, circa 1949. *Courtesy Orange County Archives.*

Orange County Fair buildings, October 1952. *Courtesy Orange County Archives.*

Then the *Los Angeles Times* reported on August 18:

> *Opening-day crowds jammed through the gates of the Orange County Fair today to see the transformation of a former Army base to a typical country fair of livestock, fruit, farm craft and civic exhibits. Manager LA Dan patch and his staff made ingenious use of facilities remaining on the old sent an army base-parade grounds in the parking lots, gymnasium into exhibit space, barracks into youth displays, drill areas into a spacious horse arena and Red Cross theater into a photographic salon. Unexpectedly large first crowds sport promise of a new attendance record for the fair which closes Sunday night.*

Orange County Fair exhibit, 1949. *Courtesy Orange County Archives.*

This photo was taken at the home show, advertising the upcoming 1949 Orange County Fair. *Courtesy Orange County Fair archives.*

Taking over the army base had been a monumental task, but it proved to be a brilliant idea. After approval by the war assets administration, the state, as associates, authorized purchase of fairgrounds with state funds. The property was appraised at $260,000, with the fair board agreeing to pay half of the appraised value. Few changes were made to the structures for the first fair. Large tents were rented for additional space in conjunction with the gymnasium. Sixth buildings were sold and removed from the property, and most of the remainder were remodeled to serve as exhibit buildings. Improvements included $80,000 for remodeling the former gymnasium, which became the agricultural building.

A total of more than $35,000 in awards was given out to exhibitors in a wide variety of classifications. Dr. Koentopp's oranges took first place in produce and the Magnolia Farm Bureau Center took first in feature exhibits open to the Farm Bureau and orange units.

With a new permanent home, the Orange County Fair as many today know it truly began to take shape.

Chapter 5

THE 1950s

N ow with a home with which to lay down true stakes in the community, the Orange County Fair got off with a bang in the 1950s.

The 1950 fair was held from August 16 to August 20 and was ushered in with an impressive show by the El Toro Marine Band. Helen Weir of Anaheim, seventeen, was crowned the queen in a year when the fair theme was "Queen of the Fair." The grand champion steer owned by Wayne Schultz sold for $1.05 per pound, bringing a total of $987. There was even the birth of a calf during the fair.

The August 20, 1950 edition of the *Los Angeles Times* reported:

> *Pres. H Clay Kellogg tonight said all-time attendance marks for the Orange County Fair were broken today and the closing crowds tomorrow are certain to push the total past the 100,000 mark, a gain of at least 25% over last year. Starting with an opening-day crowd of 18,000 Wednesday, the attendance reached 22,000 Thursday, 25,000 yesterday and was expected to top 30,000 today and tomorrow. The 1949 pick figure was 70,000.*

The 1951 event again was held in mid-August, with a "Carnival" theme, and local 4-H members took home forty ribbons in competition. Over the course of the five-day event, fair attendance records once again were shattered, breaking the former record of 97,500. For the first time ever, the fair also featured ostrich races.

The USMC band at the Orange County Fair entrance, August 1950. *Courtesy Orange County Archives.*

Brenda Joyce and H. Clay Kellogg, Orange County Fair, 1950. *Courtesy Orange County Archives.*

Stables at Orange County Fair, August 1950. *Courtesy Orange County Archives.*

A 4-H event, Orange County Fair. *Courtesy Orange County Archives.*

THE ORANGE COUNTY FAIR

The *Los Angeles Times* reported on August 19, 1951:

> *Orange County's largest and most successful fair closed tonight with the new attendance mark of about 100,000 visitors. Each day topped the comparative day of last year in total admissions, gate receipts and/or show attendance, secretary manager R.M.C. Fullenwider disclosed. The total reached 77,000 last night, after four days, not far from the five-day total of 85,000 established last year. The big steak stake events were scheduled at tonight's closing performance of the national horse show. Perhaps the most popular event was the ostrich races in which four of the big birds were trained to race with sulky carts. Arena crowds were up 54% over 1950. Entries almost doubled those of last year, and most exhibits required expanded display facilities. Featured agricultural displays were shown in the remodeled Army gymnasium which will be used year round for conventions, meetings and exhibits.*

Orange County Fair official interviewed on KFI radio, 1951. *Courtesy Orange County Fair archives.*

A competition guidebook from the 1952 Orange County Fair. *Courtesy Orange County Fair archives.*

Orange County
FAIR

Where The
Riches of the Land
Meet The
Wealth of the Sea

PREMIUM LIST

AUGUST 11-12-13-14-15-16
1953

FAIR GROUNDS
20391 NEWPORT BLVD.

SANTA ANA, CALIFORNIA

Former Santa Ana Army Air Base
(On Highway 55 at the Edge of Costa Mesa)
Between Santa Ana and Newport Beach

ENTRIES CLOSE JULY 27

A competition guidebook from the 1953 Orange County Fair. *Courtesy Orange County Fair archives.*

Fairs in 1952 and 1953 featured a "Port-O-Plenty" nautical theme. Along with the usual stellar entertainment, twelve buildings were both moved and remodeled in anticipation of the 1952 fair. The $60,000 investment was the beginning of a host of new changes that the grounds would be incorporating over the years. Also, the Orange County District of California Garden Clubs Inc. applied to the board for use of one barracks building and surrounding grounds to develop the Memorial Garden in honor of the airbase.

The 1954 theme was "Accent on Youth," and this fair featured many young performers and exhibitors. In the agriculture tent, entrants included cotton and alfalfa from Imperial County; avocados from San Diego County; and lemons, oranges and grapefruits from Riverside and Orange Counties. Orange County was the top citrus-producing county in the state with 5 million orange trees. And there was a unique promotion sponsored by the Rendezvous Ballroom in nearby Newport Beach: a chance to sail with actor James Cagney. All in all, there were 5,500 entries from 1,700 exhibitors, and the Junior Fair was one of the biggest in the state, attracting 700 4-H and FFA (Future Farmers of America) participants entering more than 2000 exhibits. Truly the youth theme was honored this year.

The Orange County Fair, circa 1950s. *Courtesy Orange County Archives.*

Orange County Fair exhibit, circa 1952. *Courtesy Orange County Archives.*

There was a bit of scandal of the 1955 fair, held from August 9 through August 14. The queen that year was sixteen-year-old Yvonne Schubert. Shortly after winning, though, she deserted the fair and was replaced by Marjorie Boyd of Anaheim. Apparently, movie mogul Howard Hughes had developed an interest in Ms. Schubert and offered her a $150-per-week movie contract in Hollywood. So she left Orange County and headed for the bright lights of showbiz. Hughes reportedly became obsessed with her and was heartbroken when the relationship ended a year or so later. She would go on to develop a career as a singer and actress. Back at the fair, it was another big year, featuring performances by big bands and a pirate band and the state baton twirling contest. This year, five two-story barracks were sliced lengthwise, and their roofed second floors were put on foundations to become one-story buildings grouped west of the administration building. The first floors were demolished to make way for the thirty-eight-thousand-square-foot Commerce Building, which at the time was the largest building of its type in Orange County.

The *Los Angeles Times* reported on the 1955 fair:

> *Record entries in the Junior livestock show and other departments of the Orange County Fair were being set up this weekend in preparation for the 63rd anniversary exposition opening on the 175 acre fairgrounds here Tuesday. The six-day fair opens Tuesday morning, centering around $250,000*

Orange County Fair flag raising, July 19, 1949. *Courtesy Orange County Archives.*

football field sized exhibits building. Extra tents were provided when flower and feature exhibits exceeded the usual space and a new elaborate entrance gate was built to permit expansion of military exhibits. Other fair features include the national horse show, the free evening pageant with 80 in the cast, model railroads, California baton twirling championships

A 4-H member pictured with his grand champion steer. *Courtesy Orange County Fair archives.*

with the finals closing night, and Sunday, August 14 there will be pogo stick races, gem show and display of fivescore paintings. Daily painting demonstrations will begin by John Hilton of Twentynine Palms, noted as an artist, historian, mineralogist, folk song singer, author and explorer. He has painted at the fair for several years adjacent to the fine arts building in the new Artcraft center.

The 1956 fair featured a Cold War icon—an actual Nike missile station on display—and a man demonstrated how the antiaircraft guided missiles worked and how they were fueled. Janice Johnson of Garden Grove, eighteen, was crowned queen, and entertainment that year featured Lawrence Welk and His Orchestra, the Hoosier Hotshots and Spade Cooley and His Orchestra. Orange County's 4-H had its most successful year ever. More than 350 youths entered and presented one hundred varieties of processes and demonstrations. This was also the first year the turnstiles were installed at the fair.

Orange County Fair, Costa Mesa, 1956. *Courtesy Orange County Archives.*

Orange County Fair citrus exhibit, circa 1940s. *Courtesy Orange County Fair archives.*

Joanne Cangi, 1953 Orange County Fair queen, from Garden Grove. *Courtesy Orange County Fair archives.*

The 1957 fair featured movie star Tab Hunter as one of the judges to select Miss Orange County on opening day. There were also rodeos, horse shows, calypso singers and the Pirate Queen contest, along with four barbershop harmony shows. Bringing a bit of high tech to the fair, a group of physicians studied X-rays, reading five thousand free X-rays taken of guests who volunteered.

The 1958 Orange County Fair was moved to earlier in the summer, from May 23 to June 1. The *Los Angeles Times* reported on May 31:

A 15-year-old farm girl who sold her prize beef for $1479 and two youthful mothers who outbaked their rivals in the orange pie and cake contest today were honored as the Orange County Fair moved into its closing weekend. The fair closes tomorrow night. Mrs. A.J. Hays of Santa Ana, mother of four, won the pie contest with a recipe handed down from her mother. Mrs. DR Smith of Anaheim, librarian and mother of two, was the cake champion. Each received a gas range. Deanne Durling, Orange high school sophomore and a member of the Villa Park Eager Beavers 4H club, topped the junior livestock auction bids with a price of $1.50 per pound for 986

Orange county Fair exhibit, circa 1953. *Courtesy Orange County Archives.*

Los Angeles County Fair Table Praise Avocados exhibit, circa 1950s. *Courtesy Orange County Fair archives.*

Orange County Fair, Casper family exhibit, circa 1950. *Courtesy Orange County Archives.*

pound Hereford steer that had already taken best 4-H honors and then the best in show award. A bid of $.50 per pound bought the reserve champion beef for $545 from Marlis Helton of Orange. The grand champion land entered by Joanne Anderson of Fullerton sold for $1.90 per pound, with the reserve champion of William Bowman of Fullerton selling for $.50. The grand champion market hog of George Strouder of Anaheim sold for $.50 per pound.

There was some controversy at this fair as well . An anonymous tip led the fair management to realize that newly crowned fair queen Linda Holmes actually lived two-tenths of a mile inside Los Angeles County. Linda was allowed to keep her crown but lost it again just two months later when it was learned that she was secretly married.

Closing out the decade in July was a fair that was themed "Better Living through Agricultural, Industrial and Educational Living." One Anaheim woman went home with seventy-two homemaking wins, a new record. The Orange County Tuberculosis and Health Association set up a free X-ray booth at the fair. This year, two helicopters also gave fairgoers sightseeing tours of the fairgrounds, and a new livestock arena and livestock building were debuted. The gem and mineral show got its own building this year, and the Orange County fishing derby offered as first prize a two-bedroom house worth $5,000 that was on display in Main Mall—it was one of the fair's most popular attractions. Food booths were another new addition to the fair, offering imported foods from Mexico. Irving Chapman, president of the fair board, noted, "This year the fair will attempt to capture the old-time quiet mood when this area was a rural one, before it became the hub of an expanding industrial empire."

Chapter 6

THE 1960s

The 1960 edition of the Orange County Fair took place from July 12 to July 17 and had a "Hawaiian Holidays" theme. The *Los Angeles Times* covered the opening:

> The annual Orange County Fair, featuring a colorful Hawaiian theme, opened Tuesday for a six-day run in the fairgrounds here. Attendance was expected to exceed last year's record of 103,000, according to officials. Highlights of the fair include a rodeo Saturday and Sunday, a Hawaiian Village made up of food and display stands and a lavishly decorated floral Pavilion staged by Harry and Josephine Macres. Macres, who was manager-designer for the recent world flower and gardenia show in the Pan Pacific Auditorium in Los Angeles, said more than 100,000 flowers were used in the floral Pavilion. A livestock auction or show and pie and cake baking contests also are included in the fair's program.

The Pirate Queen this year was Cindy Gillett of Orange. Hilo Hattie, the famed Hawaiian singer, hula dancer, actress and comedian, was here in her Hawaiian revue. Also, Robert Rockwell, who played Mr. Boynton from the *Our Miss Brooks* television series, was the grand marshal and was also on hand to announce the Santa Ana rodeo. One of the more popular attractions this year was Hugo Zacchini, also known as the human cannonball. Zacchini was actually the first human cannonball in history, as one of the Zacchini Brothers. It had been his father, Ildebrando Zacchini, who had actually invented the

Three 4-H members at an agricultural display table, circa 1950s. *Courtesy Orange County Fair archives.*

compressed air cannon used to propel humans and circus acts. By now, legendary acts like this were commonplace at the Orange County Fair.

In November 1960, a plan was put in place to improve the fairgrounds under a five-year program that was to cost more than $600,000. The enhancements included an architectural exhibits building, a floriculture pavilion, a craft center exhibit building, a horse show arena and an enlargement of the amphitheater. Also planned in the improvements were picnic tables, barbecue shelters and playground equipment for a 7.5-acre public picnic area; renovation of horse barns; stucco of wood frame buildings; public parking entrance floodlights and paving; additional fencing of property; landscaping; and resurfacing of fairground streets. The new Junior Exhibit Building was also slated to be finished for use during the 1961 fair the following July.

The "Hawaiian Holidays" theme was continued for the 1962 fair, which took place from July 10 to July 15. Hilo Hattie was back by popular demand for the third year in a row, and there was also a world championship RCA rodeo. Mrs. Ronald L. Pearson took "best in show"

Orange County Fair, circa 1960s. *Courtesy Orange County Archives.*

watercolor in the fine arts competition, and this year introduced "Every Day Is Kids Day," with kids under twelve getting attendance free with an adult. The popular Stan Volera (aka "the Man on the Swaying Pole") was a huge hit this particular year. Interestingly, at this year's fair, three trucks bringing a baby animal show to perform at the fair got lost and inadvertently wound up at the National Orange Show in San Bernardino, where it performed instead.

The 1963 Orange County Fair got rave reviews from the *Los Angeles Times* as it kicked off:

> *The action-packed 1963 Orange County Fair is off to a flying start and will continue through Sunday at the fairgrounds here. Pretty Charlene Jacobs Orange is reigning as Aloha queen. She was awarded the title in judging Tuesday night. Serving as her princesses are Christi Flinchbau of Garden Grove and Cherie Hamilton of Anaheim, who represented the city of Stanton in the contest.*

Some other highlights this year, which was again themed "Hawaiian Holidays," was the Hilo Hattie Hawaiian holiday show and the Bake-a-Cake contest sponsored by South County Gas Company; the Memorial Garden was also declared a bird sanctuary by Costa Mesa City Council

The Sheriff Department display, Orange County Fair, 1962. *Courtesy Orange County Archives.*

resolution. Also on hand was the company PacBell, which displayed a futuristic push-button phone. Over in the livestock auction, fifteen-year-old Jan Danken won for raising the "Grand Champion of Show," which sold for $5,435.

The 1964 fair, held from July 14 to July 19, had a "Diamond Jubilee of Country" theme and featured the usual top-notch lineup of entertainment. There was a Diamond Jubilee variety show in honor of Orange County's seventy-fifth-anniversary celebration, and agriculture exhibits were a major thrust of this fair. There was also an "America the Beautiful" flower-themed show by the legendary floral designer Harry Macres.

The *El Sereno Star* reported on July 16:

> *Biggest Orange County Fair in history swings into action at the fairgrounds last Tuesday for a six-day run through Sunday, July 19, in a gala county "Diamond Jubilee celebration." Cool ocean breezes blow at the Costa Mesa fairgrounds to make this event an enjoyable fun-packed family holiday. Southland counties and communities of the area display assets in elaborate feature exhibit. Commercial displays pack the big New Products Pavilion. Other exhibit departments include agriculture, horticulture, home economics, hobbies, poultry, rabbits, bees and honey, industrial education, art and photo shows, and*

A program from the 1963 Orange County Fair.
Courtesy Orange County Fair archives.

a mineral and lapidary show. The spectacular flower show, one of the west's largest, spotlights this year's "America the Beautiful" theme in elaborate displays. Rare blooms from around the world and almost every state in the nation have been brought in especially for this show by producer Harry Macres, California's "Mr. Flower Show." Popular professional entertainers take the amphitheater stage for the "Diamond Jubilee Varieties" in matinee and evening shows at 2 and 8 p.m. daily.

The 1965 "Hawaiian Holidays" fair had a South Seas Village created in honor of the theme. This year, the fair was expanded to seven days, from July 26 to August 1. Once again, California's "Mr. Flower Show," Harry Macres, was back creating floral displays, elaborately themed as "Dreams and Realities."

In 1966, the *Los Angeles Times* did a preview piece on the fair:

The stage is set for the 1966 Orange County Fair which will open Tuesday for the 18th time at the county fairgrounds here. As in past years the fair will be focused on displaying the county's agricultural wealth, combined with entertainment and hundreds of exhibits of everything from the lapidary skill to photographic art. A major event on Tuesday's schedule will be the Aloha Queen contest in which more than 20 of the county's prettiest girls will compete for the title. In a repeat of last year, a senior citizens jamboree will be held Thursday with a talent show, prizes, contests and games. The new $250,000 arena will be the setting for a championship rodeo and horse shows.

The Memorial Garden at the Orange County Fair, mid-1950s. *Courtesy Orange County Fair archives.*

Once again, the theme was "Hawaiian Holidays." The Aloha Queen was Sue Bruderlin of Huntington Beach, and there was a new rodeo arena unveiled with a covered grandstand. There was also a new livestock arena, which now holds 4,500 people.

The "Hawaiian Holidays" theme proved to be popular, as it was back yet again in 1967. The Aloha Queen was Marcia Bennett of Laguna Beach, and entertainment included veteran motion picture, radio and TV star Pat Butram as the emcee for the variety show. There was also a fire eater, Polynesian dancers and the champion R.C.A. rodeo, along with Miss Jan, the popular high-flying trapeze artist. In honor of the burgeoning space program, there was a new NASA space exhibit with a life-size replica of the *Mercury* spacecraft. It was also at this fair that the $100,000 Macres Horticulture building was dedicated in honor of the famed flower man.

After the fair that year, in October, the Pacific Jazz Festival was held at the Orange County Fairgrounds, and it featured many big names, from Duke Ellington and Muddy Waters to Joe Turner and Paul Butterfield.

A futuristic theme, "Yesterday Meets Tomorrow," was the highlight of the 1968 fair, held from July 16 to July 21. The six-day fair brought in more than 175,000 people—it was the first new theme after ten years of "Hawaiian

17th ANNUAL
ORANGE COUNTY
FAIR
JULY 27
thru
AUGUST 1
1965
COSTA MESA, CALIFORNIA

HAWAIIAN
HOLIDAYS

JUNE LINDEMAN
1964 ALOHA QUEEN

A program from the 1965 Orange County Fair.
Courtesy Orange County Fair archives.

Holidays." Entertainment included Glenn Campbell, the Up with People singers, the Barbershop Quartet Jamboree, the Kingsmen and the National Champion Drum and Bugle Corps, among others. The popular tightrope artist Monty Montana performed, and there was a new feature exhibit about boats and recreational vehicles. Also, an all-time record was set by a Future Farmers of America student: the lamb of Jona Ronan of La Habra, "Dick," was the grand champion of the fair.

A few weeks after the fair, in 1968, the music landscape in Orange County changed at the site of the fairgrounds as the Newport Pop Festival rolled in. Not only was it the first concert ever have more than 100,000 paid attendees, but it was also one of the first major music festivals ever to be held in Southern California.

Organized by twenty-six-year-old Gary Schmitt and his father, Al, the festival was originally said to be held inside the actual fairgrounds in an outdoor pavilion. But once everyone got a sense of how many people would be attending in the days leading up to the show, the decision was made to move the festival to twenty adjoining parking lots. This meant that there would be no shade for attendees, and there was also a mad scramble to move all of the fencing, staging, sanitation and food concessions to the new area. As a result, things did not go as smoothly as originally planned. But the lineup was incredibly impressive, and many fans today have fond memories of the festival.

Today, Gary Schmitt makes his home in Nevada. When asked with a few of his favorite memories were from that weekend, he offered, "Taking Marty Balin and Grace Slick in a ride over the event in the helicopter, along with the Chambers brothers and Eric Burdon. There is film available online now. My photos burned up in an album in a house fire, but I still have the negatives somewhere but have not found them yet."

This was how the event was covered by *Rolling Stone* magazine:

Newport Pop Festival Drags on in Dust and Heat: Dead, Country Joe, Crosby, Pie Fight Weekend's Highlights:

- *An estimated 140,000 attended the first and probably the last Newport Pop Festival in California's Orange County Aug 3–4, viewing, among others, Tiny Tim, Jefferson Airplane, Country Joe and the Fish, Grateful Dead, Chambers Brothers, Charles Lloyd, James Cotton Blues Band, Quicksilver Messenger Service, and the Byrds.*

A program from the 1968 Orange County Fair.
Courtesy Orange County Fair archives.

- *The festival was regarded musically successful but on other fronts rather less than pleasing. The performers appeared on a raised stage under a striped canopy, but the young crowds were left sitting or standing in a huge, flat, dusty-dry open field under a broiling sun. Refreshment and rest room facilities were less than adequate and the sound system was not powerful enough to carry the sound to everyone present.*

- *The highlight of the pop fest on the first day (Saturday) seemed to come when Country Joe closed the bill. The hour was late and Orange County officials were threatening to shut off the electricity when the band went on, finally relenting to give the band time for two songs. As they began their first, "1, 2, 3, 4, What Are We Fighting For," the approximately 40,000 young people still on hand rose as if one, cheering, hands held aloft in the "peace sign." During the second number, a long blues, even the cops on stage were grinning and adlibbing a moderate version of the boogaloo.*

- *The second day's climax came when David Crosby started a planned pie fight with Jefferson Airplane. In all, 250 cream pies flew back and forth…and the thousands of people present stormed the stage to join in.*

- *The musical line-up was an impressive one. Besides those already mentioned, bands appearing were Alice Cooper, Steppenwolf, Sonny and Cher, Canned Heat, Electric Flag, Butterfield Blues Band, Eric Burdon and the Animals, Blue Cheer, Iron Butterfly, Illinois Speed Press and Things to Come.*

- *But admission to the festival was $5.50 per day—to sit in heat and dust. Most considered it another in the series of pop music shucks.*

- *The Newport Pop Festival—which wasn't even held in Newport, but in Costa Mesa—was produced by Humble Harvey Miller, one of L.A.'s Top-40 DJs, and Wesco Associates, basically the same coalition that staged a similarly uncomfortable weekend festival last summer in another Los Angeles dust bin.*

Three days after the event, the Costa Mesa City Council decided that there would not be a Newport Pop Festival encore. "To say that we would not like it back here would be the understatement of the year," Costa Mesa mayor Alvin Pinkley was quoted as saying.

The decade closed out with the 1969 fair, held from July 15 to July 20. The theme was "Fiesta Fun," and Miss Orange County Fair for 1969 was Linda Paris of Fullerton, eighteen. The Rodeo Queen was Julie Cordell, and entertainment included singer Lou Rawls; Florenzio Yescas, a ballet dancer; the Popcorn Theater Puppeteers; and jazz artist Don Ellis. There was even a space show in honor of the first moon landing, featuring a one-third scale model moonwalk at the fairground. The grand champion pig was "Cecil," raised by Cynthia Dunham of 4-H in Yorba Linda. Motorcycle speedway racing was kicked off at the fair and continued through the fall months in the grandstand arena.

Chapter 7

THE 1970s

The first fair of the new decade kicked off with a "County Fun" theme and was held from July 14 to July 19. There was entertainment provided by Hank Thompson and the Brazos Valley Boys, singer Curtis Potter and county singing star Ferlin Husky. Children were admitted free on July 16, and Jill Shelton of Seal Beach was crowned queen. James Drury, star of the TV show *The Virginian*, appeared at the rodeo. The Memorial Garden and adjacent building were recognized as some of Orange County's first points of historical interest. Also this year, a rock-and-roll version of "The Star-Spangled Banner" was performed without permission by an unpaid young band that had not even been hired by the fair. Complaints from fairgoers caused such a controversy that, for a time, management banned rock music from the fair.

The theme in 1971 was "Something for Everyone," and the six-day run, from July 13 to July 18, set an attendance record of 105,000 people. Janet Hagemeier from La Palma, nineteen, was crowned queen, and entertainment this year included the American National Circus, and the Pat Boone family headlined opening night. Jo Ann Castle, from *The Lawrence Welk* TV show, also made an appearance. It was also this year that the fair board began discussing plans to sell thirty-three acres of land to raise money for improvements at the fair. However, Costa Mesa City Council, believing that the highest bids would be from housing developers, froze the property and zoned for institutional or recreational use. Attendance just continued to grow throughout the decade.

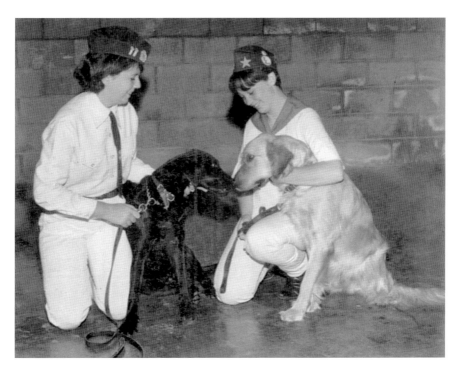

A 1970 4-H guide dog program. *Courtesy Orange County Fair archives.*

The 1972 fair was themed "Action '72" and was held from June 16 to July 25. This year, attendance jumped to 248,439. This was the first ten-day fair and included performances by the Everly Brothers, a youth circus and country western performers Eddie Dean & Dorsey Burnett; interestingly, the first-ever postage stamp created by a county fair was debuted. There was even a special post office at the fair to postmark envelopes. In addition to a country western show, there was also a jet aircraft display featuring a T-37 military trainer. June 22 was Armed Forces Appreciation Day, and all service men and women in uniform were admitted free. This was also the last time the fair was held in June until the present day. The reason the schedule was changed this year was to avoid conflict with the Del Mar Fair, located a few hours south near San Diego.

The 1973 fair had the theme of "Good Old Days '73." The theme stuck around through 1976. Attendance took an astounding leap to just under 150,000 people—a 40 percent increase over the year before. The huge uptick in attendees was attributed to the fact that it was the first time that the fair implemented a one-pay gate system. Now, all attractions, stage shows,

Above: One of the rare postmarked envelopes from the 1972 Orange County Fair, from a time when it actually had a special post office installed. *Courtesy Orange County Fair archives.*

Left: A program from the 1976 Orange County Fair. *Courtesy Orange County Fair archives.*

exhibits, rodeo and motorcycle races were all available under one general admission price.

Entertainment this year included the Red Buttons Band, Les Brown, Freddie Martin and His Orchestra and the Coasters. There was even a first "Diaper Derby" where boys and girls six months to fifteen months competed for first place in several categories. The challenge was that they had to crawl during the race, with no standing or walking. The queen this year was Marian Sammons from Huntington Beach, seventeen. The media coverage was getting more advanced, too. Opening-day ceremonies were televised on Channel 9, KHJ TV, for three hours. Regis Philbin was the host of the program, which aired on July 6.

The crowds just kept on coming. The 1974 fair, held from July 12 through July 21, had the theme of "Good Old Days '74." Once again, it was a ten-day event, and attendance was an astounding 213,000 people. Entertainment this year included the Four Freshmen, the Grassroots, Hank Thompson and the Brazos Valley Boys, the Harborlites Chorus and the Staple Singers. The fair queen in 1974 was Diane Culp, seventeen, who was also crowned Miss Fullerton that year.

The theme of "Good Old Days" continued in 1975, and attendance continued to grow. Sheri Chiesa of Huntington Beach, nineteen, was crowned queen. The entertainment lineup included Bob Hope, Les Brown, Rosemary Clooney, the rock group Sugarloaf and the Orange County Boys Choir, among many others. There was also a skateboard riding contest, a chili eating contest and the fair's very first wedding ceremony, which featured Preston Hibbard, the fair's art director, and his assistant, Dixie Lee, who were married at the Flower and Garden show on July 16. There was also Mexican-American Day on July 16, which featured special performances by Mexican entertainers, including Gloria Eva and Frederico Vasquez. Later this year, the Great Earth Festival took place during autumn to test the feasibility of a fall fair. Country singers appeared at this event, which was held on the carnival lot, with the audience sitting on bales of hay. A haystack and huge sand pile for children on the center mall was included with the crafts exhibit.

Of course, the bicentennial fair, held from July 16 through July 25, featured lots of patriotic displays and a special salute to Orange County's heritage. Teri Daniels of Garden Grove, nineteen, was crowned queen, and she later became Miss Garden Grove and Miss Orange County Universe. The solid entertainment lineup this year included Marty Robbins, Steppin' Stones, the Strangers, Andy Russell and a ten-year-old fiddle player named

Tiger Bill. Bob Hope also came back to entertain. There was a symphony concert on July 25, along with motorcycle races and a Sculpture Invitational featured in the Fine Arts Building. For the first time, the fair featured the Children's Hospital of Orange County (CHOC) healthcare display; camera and model day on July 17, whereby thirty girls had a chance to model; and Chef Frank Moser demonstrating easy ways to cook with eggs. In the livestock competition, awards for grand champion market animals went to Mary Ann Wharton Berger of Fullerton for her 150-pound lamb. The blue ribbon animals were sold in an auction, which ended with a total of $117,398 and proceeds for the participating 4-H and Future Farmers of America groups.

An image from the 1979 Orange County Fair. A contest was held to find a name for the chicken mascot this year. *Courtesy Orange County Fair archives.*

The 1977 theme, "The Orange County Fair Comes Alive," held from July 15 through July 24, seems to have been inspired by the popular Peter Frampton album of the day, *Frampton Comes Alive*. Big-name performers this year included Roy Rogers and Dale Evans, the Hudson Brothers, Jose Feliciano, George Benson, Kenny Rogers and Jim Stafford, among many others. And there was a new event, the literary competition, sponsored by the Orange County Fair for ages seventeen and younger, with categories including writing, illustrating and more.

In 1978, the theme of the fair was "Home Grown," and it was held from July 17 to July 23. This year, just under 250,000 people came to the fair. The queen this year with Suzanne Rubio from Costa Mesa, and entertainment included the Lawrence Welk singers, Elvin

Bishop, Eddie Rabbit, the Chinese Circus of Taiwan and B.J. Thomas, among others. There was a "Focus at the Fair" photography competition that was open to any local resident visiting the fair's army exhibit. The fair also featured the first annual Run for Your Life, a 7.5-mile run through the city of Costa Mesa. In addition to the second annual commercial and homemade wine show, there was also a tribute to Harry Macres, known as "Mr. Flower Show," who had managed the floriculture building since the late 1940s.

The 1970s ended with a fair that was themed "A Touch of Country" and was held from July 13 to July 22, 1979. Ricky Nelson and the Stone Canyon band performed, along with Debbie Boone, Elvin Bishop and country rock star Roger Miller. There was a unique All States Reunion Day where you could register at the fifty tables from your home state and then meet for an old-fashioned picnic. Benjamin Vander Meide, known as "Europe's Fastest Hypnotist," also dazzled and amazed fairgoers. Reflecting the cultural times, there was a Disco Nights "Space Disco," along with Laser Discomania. All in all, the 1970s had been another extremely successful decade for the fair. Things just kept getting better.

Chapter 8

THE 1980s

The first fair of the new decade kicked off with the theme "A Touch of Country," and entertainment that year included the typically wide array of talent, such as Hoyt Axton, Helen Reddy, Pat Boone, Shari Lewis with Lamb Chop and the band War. The junior livestock auction brought in more than $200,000, and the new equestrian center opened, including six show rings in 276 stalls to accommodate local horse owners with boarding and training facilities. Attendance also skyrocketed to 341,000 including the all-time single-day mark of 53,875 on Saturday, July 19. What a way to start the decade.

Playing off the previous year's theme, 1981's Orange County Fair featured "There's Still a Touch of Country," with another stellar music lineup that included Rick Nelson, the Association, Bo Diddley, the Coasters, Don McLean and the Grassroots, along with emcee Dick Clark. The new queen designation was "Orange County Girl," and in 1981, it was Shannon Cleye of Newport Beach. The single-day record for attendance was broken on July 18 when 55,790 came through the turnstiles, while a fair total of 368,903 set a new total attendance record. It seemed that everything was still on its way up. There was an exhibit total of $7,644, and the livestock auction alone took in more than $170,000.

The year rolled in with an "All American Fair" theme. The entertainment this year included Bobby Vinton, Rita Coolidge, B.J. Thomas, Rain (a tribute to the Beatles), Wolfman Jack, Roy Orbison, Elvin Bishop and a host of big bands. Dufty Iyon, sculpting a cow made out of butter, used

An aerial image of the Orange County fairgrounds from 1982. *Courtesy Orange County Fair archives.*

five hundred pounds of the stuff and took two and a half days to complete his feat. Scott and Barbara Tracy renewed their wedding vows in the floriculture building, and the Fun-a-Poppin Circus gave four performances daily. Also this year, the model railroad building was razed to accommodate construction of the soon-to-be-built Pacific Amphitheatre.

The concert venue was opened in July 1983, christened with a show by Barry Manilow. With a capacity of 18,500, it saw its share of big-name shows early on. Notable is the fact that Marvin Gaye performed his last concert ever at this venue on August 14, 1983. It was during the ill-fated Sexual Healing tour, which often saw Gaye's performances affected by his heavy cocaine use. At the end of the show, the Motown legend went to live at his parents' home in Los Angeles, and on April 1 1984, Gaye died after being shot by his father. After being closed in the early '90s, the popular theater reopened in 2003 in conjunction with the fair, and it is still one of the most popular music venues in Southern California today.

The 1983 fair, held from July 8 to July 17, was themed "Everything's Coming Up Rosy." As you can guess, there were many rose-themed events

1984

In 1984, the fair became bigger than life when an inflatable, seventy-two-foot King Kong towered over the fairgrounds. *Courtesy Orange County Fair archives.*

that year. The music had a bit of a nostalgic flavor to it, with performances by the Righteous Brothers, Frankie Laine, the reunited Jan and Dean, Rick Nelson and the Kingston Trio. About 4,700 exhibitors contributed 10,225 entries, a staggering number. More than 1,800 wines were entered in a commercial wine competition, and the Orange County Fair got a new general manager this year, Norb Bartosik.

Actor Kirk Alyn was a popular attraction at the 1984 fair, which was themed "It's a Horse of a Different Color." He was the original on-screen Superman, and his autograph signings featured long lines and enthusiastic comic book fans. In addition, there was an entire Superman collection exhibit, which had more than 6 million items and was valued at more than $2 million. Another iconic figure, King Kong (or an inflatable version of him at least seventy-two feet tall), towered over the fairgrounds. Musical entertainment this year included Marie Osborne, Jan and Dean, Les Brown, Exile, the Righteous Brothers, America and Johnny Rivers, among others.

Another famed giant inflatable, this time a fifty-two-foot replica of the Statue of Liberty, was on hand for the 1985 fair, which was themed "Its Wild and Woolly." The inflatable statue was there to commemorate the restoration that year of the grand lady in New York City. There was also another customer wedding. Julie Dixon, twenty, got married on her favorite ride, the Sea Dragon, to John Knutson, twenty-three. And for the first time ever, the fair brought in more than $1 million in admission thanks to a paid attendance record of 362,907. It seems that every year, things grew bigger and better for the Orange County Fair.

The year 1986 was themed "Jump on Over," and true to form, the attendance record was shattered once again. There was also special appearance by Father Mac, the "Carny Priest," a man of faith who took religion on the road for carnival workers. The monsignor, whose full name is Robert McCarthy, celebrated mass one morning under the roller coaster in a special service blessing the fair. Living out of a suitcase just like the carnies he served for so long, McCarthy stated, "I will set up wherever I can to be heard." In 1979, Father Mac had been honored with a private audience with Pope John Paul II, who was impressed with his work with carnival and circus people.

Eggs took center stage in 1987 with the theme "Don't Miss the Egg-Citement." For the first time in fair history, the event ran for eleven days, from July 9 to July 19. On July 18, the crowd hit 73,801, an all-time mark for a single day. One of the more impressive collections this year at the fair was the First Lady's Collection, a forty-six-piece set. Each piece was hand-made

Jan and Dean perform at the 1985 Orange County Fair. *Courtesy Orange County Fair archives.*

by Beverly Mosier of Laguna Beach. In fact, Mosier hand-made everything in the collection, including dolls wearing exact replicas of dresses the first ladies wore for their respective inauguration balls. Each porcelain doll was cast from molds that she made, following the descriptions of each first lady sent by the Smithsonian Institution. The music this year included performances by the Righteous Brothers, Billy Vera and the Beaters, Captain & Tennille, the Coasters, Freddy Cannon and the Shirelles.

In 1988, the fair hired a new assistant manager, Becky Bailey Findley. The daughter of longtime fair employee Jim Bailey, she would one day go on to be the CEO of the fair. "We're Beefin' It Up" was the theme in 1988, and the Orange County Fair mascot was a 2,300-pound, twenty-one-month-old Chianina bull from Chino. Skydivers dropped in from the sky on opening day for the more than fifteen thousand guests who attended. Music this year included Paul Revere and the Raiders, Mary Welles, Dick Dale and the Deltones, Elvin Bishop, Steppenwolf and the Gatlin Brothers, among others.

The last fair of the 1980s took place from July 12 to July 23, and the theme was "Stop and Smell the Flowers." The official mascot was "Blossom

Becky Bailey (Findley), future Orange County Fair CEO. *Courtesy Orange County Fair archives.*

the rabbit," and the fair's first commemorative print—"Orange County Squeeze" by lithograph artist Mary Ellen Wehrli—was put on display. The lithograph combined both the county's population and building explosions by depicting six rabbits peeking out of six stacked boxes. Also that year, the rat and mouse exhibit was one of the more popular attractions of the entire fair. Performers included Three Dog Night, Rita Coolidge, Tony Orlando and Dawn and Johnny Cash with June Carter, among others.

Chapter 9

THE 1990s

In 1990, the theme of the fair was "Very Berry Extraordinary." This year, the Orange County Fair saluted pigs and strawberries. Shortcake, the 450-pound Yorkshire-Hampshire pig, became a celebrity with her piglets in Centennial Farm, a new attraction. Centennial Farm was partly inspired by the efforts of Jim Bailey, longtime livestock supervisor at the fair. The farm, featuring farm animals and crops, almost automatically became a must-see attraction. Here is how the *Los Angeles Times* described the farm at its opening:

Crops of peanuts, kiwis and rhubarb—rarely seen in Orange County—mingle with the traditional crops of corn and lima beans on a small farm in the middle of urban Costa Mesa. The unusual crops were planted because the children who visit this one-acre farm on the Orange County Fairgrounds are fascinated by them, supervisor Kevin Arnett said. And this farm exists to fascinate children.

Centennial Farm was an employee parking lot in the corner of the fairgrounds when fair officials decided to turn it into an educational tool. Tours of students and adults come through three times a day now to see something that is rapidly disappearing from urban Orange County.

"We grow everything," Arnett said. "Anything we can try to grow, we grow because of the interest to our kids."

On the tours, guides usually ask the children where they think bread or Cheerios come from. The children usually can trace their food only as far as the store, Arnett said.

A promotional sticker from the 1990 Orange County Fair featuring Shortcake the Yorkshire crossbreed pig. *Courtesy Orange County Fair archives.*

About 25 to 30 crops are rotated as the seasons change, Arnett said. Eggplants the size of small onions are starting to hang over their wire supports and bright orange pumpkins look ready to take away.

Most of the crops have historical significance, Arnett said. "Lima beans at one time were the number one crop in Orange County and strawberries are now the number two crop."

Today, hundreds of thousands of children have visited Centennial Farm both during the fair and also during off-season periods, and it remains one of the fair's most popular attractions.

A display about the fair's history was on exhibit at the 1991 Orange County Fair. *Courtesy Orange County Archives.*

Also at the 1990 fair, there was a lumberjack show and an unusual newspaper toss contest, and the commemorative artist Robert Marble unveiled the print titled *Strawberry Short Pigs*. Entertainment this year included Melissa Manchester, Glen Campbell, Pat Boone, Frankie Avalon and Annette Funicello. A record attendance of 555,106 verified the wild, enduring popularity of the Orange County Fair.

Another big new attraction was unveiled in 1991: Centennial Hall. It included historic exhibits of the past ninety-nine years of the Orange County Fair, including historical developments of the fair, photos and memorabilia. The theme this year was "How Sweet It Is," a salute to the bee and honey industries. History was made when Dr. Norm Gray, an entomologist from University of California–Davis, performed daily in the arena, covering his body with pheromones (the perfume of the queen bee), resulting in several hundred thousand bees covering his body, while he played the clarinet in the key of B. He also designed working beehives that were viewed through Plexiglas. It remains one of the great photo opportunities in Orange County Fair history. Additionally, at the '91 fair, there were contests that included a beehive hairdo contest, saying "bumblebee" with a mouth full of marshmallows and more. A wine pavilion also premiered this year. Of

Perhaps Patrick O'Donnell's most famous shot: entomologist Norm Gray at the 1991 Orange County Fair. *Courtesy Orange County Fair archives.*

course, attendance records were broken yet again on eleven of the twelve days for a grand total of 637,014 attendees between July 17 and July 28.

In 1992, in honor of the fair's centennial, the county's one-hundred-year-old residents were saluted. The theme this year was "Meet Our Main Squeeze," along with "100 Years in the Making: The OC Fair

Centennial Experience." This was also the last year for entertainment in the Arlington Theater.

In 1993, the fair marked the 100th anniversary of the Ferris wheel with a record-breaking thirty-eight-day Ferris wheel ride by Jeff Block of Tustin. In honor of the anniversary, the theme (along with "We're Having Bushels of Fun") was "It's the Wheel Thing."

In 1994, an authentic cattle drive down Fairview Road was staged with more than 125 riders and 250 head of cattle. The Pacific Amphitheatre was closed for the first time since opening in 1983. Several horse shows delighted guests, and "Becky" the buffalo became the newest addition to the Centennial Farm. The *Los Angeles Times* saw the '94 fair like this:

> *FREEWAY COWBOYS: This year's Orange County Fair, which opens Friday and runs through July 24, is called "Saddle Up for Fun," and for good reason. Not only are there a rodeo and scads of horse shows, but on July 15, 250 head of cattle will be led down Fairview Road to the Costa Mesa fairgrounds from Costa Mesa High School, two blocks away. Los Angeles lawyer Eugene Veenhuis, who owns a Montana cattle ranch, will be among the 100-plus guest riders.... "It'll be great fun," he says. "With about one rider for every two cows, we shouldn't have too much problem with any of them running off down the street."*
>
> *PRETTY FAIR STATS: Last year's total fair attendance was 668,096, down slightly from 1992's heavily promoted 100th anniversary event but in line with previous years....Among last year's big numbers: 56,000 ears of corn were eaten, 43,000 people tried the "Footsie Wootsie" foot massager, 31,000 visited the traditional log cabin, and 15,000 rode the elephant...To avoid the crowds, try a day besides Saturday. Last year's two Saturdays drew almost 20% of the 17-day attendance.*

In 1995, a five-thousand-square-foot rainforest called "Thunder Lagoon" was featured, including a waterfall depicting a tropical terrain that was created to match that fair's theme of "Come to Our Garden Party." To give one an idea of just how diverse and varied the fair had become by now, here is a breakdown of events for this year, as provided by the Orange County Fair:

A HISTORY OF CELEBRATION

* FRIDAY
Theme: Kids' Day (children under twelve admitted free), also Harley-Davidson Day (Arlington Theater)
9:30 a.m., outside main gate: opening ceremonies with live music.
7:30 p.m., Pacific Amphitheatre: Ricky Van Shelton (country).

* SATURDAY
Theme: Harley-Davidson Day (Arlington Theater)
7:30 p.m., Pacific Amphitheatre: Stephen Stills (folk/blues/rock).
8:00 p.m., Grand Stand Arena: sidecar/quad racing.

* SUNDAY
Theme: Cars of the Past and Future (Arlington Theater)
3:00 p.m., Equestrian Center: Pacific Coast Quarter Horse Assocation Horse Show.
4:00 p.m., Centennial Stage: Babylon Mood (belly dance troupe).
7:30 p.m., Pacific Amphitheatre: Shenandoah (country).
8:00 p.m., Grand Stand Arena: midget car races.

* MONDAY
Theme: Teens' Day (ages thirteen through seventeen admitted for three dollars), also Water Sports Day (Arlington Theater)
1:00 p.m.–6:00 p.m., Grand Stand Arena: Youth Motorized Olympics.
7:30 p.m., Pacific Amphitheatre: All 4 One (R&B/soul).
9:30 p.m., Arlington Theater: Revels Surf Band.

* TUESDAY
Theme: Water Sports Day (Arlington Theater)
6:00 p.m. Bijou Theater: Los Estrellas Ballet Folkorico.
7:30 p.m., Pacific Amphitheatre: Melissa Manchester (pop).
7:30 p.m., Arlington Theater: Zydeco Party Band.

* WEDNESDAY
7:30 p.m., Pacific Amphitheatre: Richard Jeni (comedy).

* JULY 13
Theme: Seniors' Day (ages fifty-five and over admitted for three dollars; free Ferris wheel and carousel rides)
11:00 a.m., Arlington Theater: Seniors' Hat Parade.

12:00 p.m., Arlington Theater: USO Show honoring World War II veterans.
7:30 p.m., Pacific Amphitheatre: Paul Revere and the Raiders (oldies rock).

* JULY 14
Theme: Kids' Day
10:30 a.m., Grand Stand Arena: Southern California Firefighter Combat Challenge.
7:30 p.m., Pacific Amphitheatre: Jamie Walters (pop/rock).

* JULY 15
Theme: Fitness Day (Arlington Theater)
9:00 a.m., Grand Stand Arena: Team penning.
7:30 p.m., Pacific Amphitheatre: Little Richard (oldies rock).

* JULY 16
Theme: Pickup Truck Day (Arlington Theater)
9:00 a.m., Grand Stand Arena: Team penning.
7:30 p.m., Pacific Amphitheatre: Woody Lee (country).

* JULY 17
Theme: Teens' Day, also Pickup Truck Day (Arlington Theater)
1:30 p.m., Fair Ring: K-9 Comets/Frisbee Dog Show.
7:30 p.m., Pacific Amphitheatre: Kool & the Gang (retro pop, dance tunes).

* JULY 18
Theme: Martial Arts Day (Arlington Theater)
7:30 p.m., Pacific Amphitheatre: Jazz Night with Richard Elliot and Craig Chaquico.

* JULY 19
Theme: Youth Ag Day (4-H and FFA members admitted free with membership card), also Environmental Awareness Day (Arlington Theater)
6:30 p.m., Arlington Theater: hypnotist Mark Yuzuik.
7:30 p.m., Pacific Amphitheatre: the Brian Setzer Orchestra (rockabilly).

* JULY 20
Theme: Seniors' Day
7:30 p.m., Pacific Amphitheatre: Marty Stuart (country).
8:00 p.m., Grand Stand Arena: Flying U Rodeo Classic.

*JULY 21
Theme: Kids' Day
7:30 p.m., Pacific Amphitheatre: the Association (oldies pop).
8:00 p.m., Grand Stand Arena: Flying U Rodeo Classic.

*JULY 22
Theme: Pet Day (Arlington Theater)
4:00 p.m. and 8:00 p.m., Coors Light Arena: Flying U Rodeo Classic.
7:30 p.m., Pacific Amphitheatre: Firehouse (hard rock).

*JULY 23
Theme: Fiesta Del Mariachi Day
4:00 p.m., Grand Stand Arena: Flying U Rodeo Classic with mariachis and Mexican rodeo events.
5:00 p.m., Arlington Theater: Mariachi Sol de Mexico.
7:30 p.m., Pacific Amphitheatre: Vikki Carr (pop tunes in English and Spanish).

In 1996, things got buggy when biologist/"Bug Chef" Ron Taylor tempted guests with insect cuisine using crickets, mealworms and other crawling critters, which perfectly fit with the theme of the year, "We're Puttin' a Bug in Your Ear," a salute to agriculture and insects.

The 1997 theme was "We're Goin' Tropical: Nuttin' but Fun!" Visitors this year were invited to relax on stretches of sand, listen to island music and eat tropical cuisine during the event lasting from July 11 to July 27. Island plant life, murals, sand sculptures and other decorative elements graced the fairgrounds, along with livestock, produce, rides, music and other agricultural mainstays that by now had become consistent parts of the Orange County Fair experience. Wacky entertainer King Kukulele and "Peanut Man" Roger Owens from Dodger Stadium were on hand to wow the crowds. This was also the first year of the Alaskan pig races.

In 1998, the fair theme, "We're in the Pink" (a salute to fuchsias and fiber arts), featured the first ever sheep drive through the streets of Costa Mesa. A zoot suit fashion show and nightly big bands invited fairgoers to swing dance at the Heritage Stage. Livestock exhibits continued to fascinate fair guests. For many years, more than two hundred 4-H and FFA animals were taken to auction. Small pets and potbellied pigs were included.

A promotional pack of watermelon seeds from the 1997 Orange County Fair. *Courtesy Orange County Fair archives.*

In 1999, the theme was "Join the Rush" (a salute to gold and grain). Led by Billy's Brass Band, a costumed cast of *The Wizard of Oz* paraded to Heritage Stage to open the fair before yet another successful decade came to a close.

Chapter 10

THE 2000s

Among the most popular attractions of the 2000s were the All-Alaskan Racing Pigs and hypnotist Mark Yuzuik, whose skills brought out the singing, dancing and star potential of selected members of his audiences. Shaded areas were extended for fairgoers' comfort. Thrill-seekers found satisfaction with the huge Euroslide and the fifteen-story-high La Grande Wheel, which provided a panoramic view of much of Orange County.

In 2000, dancing and weaving their way from the Main Gate, 150 fairgoers in Orange County's longest conga line made it a "Hot! Hot! Hot!" opening ceremony (that was also the theme this year). A "Blossom to Awesome" display related the citrus industry's local history. Millennium Barn, which at forty-seven feet became the fair's tallest building, opened in time for the 2000 fair.

In 2001 (with a theme of "Twist and Shout," which celebrated surf and sun), attendance increased to record levels in the first years of the fair's new century, growing to a new high record of 843,347 in 2001. The second Saturday of the 2001 fair also set the record for the highest single-day attendance with 84,895 (Gallagher and the demolition derby were the day's paid entertainment). Fair programmers introduced fairgoers to the Orange Crush Demolition Derby, an evening of destruction, chaos and sheer entertainment for free in the Grandstand Arena. Irvin C. Chapman—who served twenty-seven years on the fair board and whose father, C.C. Chapman, was considered the father of Orange County's Valencia orange industry—was honored during 2001 opening-day ceremonies. Offered for

Pop/comedy musician "Weird Al" Yankovic with fair staff at the "The 'Weird Al' Experience" exhibit at the Orange County Fair, Costa Mesa, July 2002. *Courtesy Orange County Archives.*

the first time, a limited number of "Orange Circle" reserved seats in the Arlington Theater allowed concertgoers to beat the crowds for a guaranteed seat at Chubby Checker, En Vogue, Hall & Oates and other performances. The 2001 fair also saluted the fiftieth anniversary of the *I Love Lucy* TV show with an interactive exhibit/museum and a Lucy look-alike contest.

"Leap into the Fair" was the theme for 2002, and a goal for the fair was to foster a sense of togetherness while paying tribute to those who serve the community. To help make that point, members of local police agencies, fire departments and a contingent of fifty marines from Camp Pendleton were honored during the day's opening ceremonies.

In 2003, the fair extended its dates to twenty-one days and welcomed concertgoers back to the Pacific Amphitheatre for the new Summer Concert Series. This first year featured performances by Dianna Krall, Duran Duran, Devo, Steely Dan, Alan Jackson, 311, 3 Doors Down and Boston. The popular Skyride also opened this year at the fair.

In 2004, grapes were celebrated with "Jammin' at the Fair: The Year of the Grape." The theme was evident in the numerous concerts, including a week devoted to tribute bands, a weeklong stay by "Weird Al" Yankovic and a weeklong

Longtime Orange County Fair Board member Emily Sanford welcomes the Carhops to the Orange County Fair, July 2003. *Courtesy Orange County Archives.*

tribute to Motown music. Grapes, the object of the 2004 fair's agricultural salute, reach California tables in three major forms and are a mainstay of the state's agricultural bounty. They are the basis of California industries for raisins, table grapes and wine and provide cottage industries for boutique jams and jellies. Vineyards cover 700,000 California acres, and 97 percent of all commercially grown U.S. table grapes come from California. Nearly half of the world's raisins come from the state's San Joaquin Valley. Grapes are the state's second-most valuable agricultural commodity at $2.58 billion. Wines are California's third-most valuable export, worth $490 million. The value of grapes is not just economic. Contemporary research showed that they are loaded with biologically active phytonutrients that fight cancer and heart disease, and so the theme that year targeted broader issues beyond just a catchy line.

In 2005, the fair broke the million-visitor mark for the first time with 1,058,192 fairgoers attending. The lucky millionth visitor, seven-year-old Rebecca Harris of Anaheim, was awarded a lifetime pass to the fair to mark the record-breaker. "It's Callin' You Out to Play: The Year of the Avocado" celebrated avocados and fun in 2005. The theme focused on the joy a child at age or heart can feel when at play. A special free play area at the main gate and a toy exhibit were added just for the theme.

From left to right: Vee Kay the Clown, soon-to-be Anaheim mayor Curt Pringle and Orange County Fair board of director Randy Smith at the Orange County Fair, Costa Mesa, in the summer of 2002. *Courtesy Orange County Archives.*

The 2006 theme of "Flower Power: The Year of the Garden" celebrated the wonder of California's flowers and produce with satellite-powered gardens, energy-efficient fuel cells and rows and rows of sweet-smelling blooms. As the *Orange County Register* wrote, "OC Reg Fair-goers anticipating the guilty pleasure of biting into the latest deep-fried indulgence at the 114th Orange County Fair this summer should brace themselves for a gut-check. The fair foodies aren't rolling out a new version of deep-fried comfort this year. With the steady diet of battered Twinkies, Oreos and Snickers that have been introduced at the fair over the past few years, it may be tough reality to swallow. This year the focus is on flowers, not frying."

The Centennial Farm this year was beautifully transformed by master gardeners, and a large group of local fifth and sixth graders planted a children's garden that will be part of the farm year-round.

Also this year, the fair saw record temperatures and offered fairgoers a "Beat the Heat" promotion with discount admission; more than thirty thousand fairgoers took advantage of the last-minute offering.

The 2007 fair started off with a cattle drive through the county to attract attention to the theme "Cowabunga!: The Year of Herefords, Surfers & Sand." People lined up to watch as one hundred steer and

The midway of the Orange County Fair, 2008.

twenty-five horses walked 1.5 miles from Golden West Street down Pacific Coast Highway and then on the sand to the site of the U.S. Open of Surfing competition. Also this year, the fair showcased two cattle drives—one on the sandy shores of Huntington Beach as part of the U.S. Open of Surfing and one in which some three hundred head of cattle were led down the streets of Costa Mesa from Fairview Park to the fair. A record 1,090,653 guests enjoyed the fair in 2007.

In 2008, the fair partnered with the Maloof Money Cup to offer three days of skateboarding and BMX competition in the Grandstand Arena. "Say Cheese!" was the theme for this year, complete with exhibits on cheese production, cheese tastings and a sculpture crafted out of a 640-pound block of cheddar. The fair also held another cattle drive through the streets of Costa Mesa.

In 2009, the fair expanded its dates to twenty-three days and introduced a self-produced, interactive exhibit called "Al's Brain: A 3-D Journey through the Human Brain with 'Weird Al' Yankovic." In its first hour, 26,202 fairgoers passed through the gate the first day. The record-breaking attendance was nearly 25 percent higher than the year before. This year, B.B. King, Chris Isaak and One Republic were the big musical headliners.

In May 2009, Governor Arnold Schwarzenegger offered a multifaceted proposal to state politicians in an effort to balance California's more than $26 billion budget deficit. In this proposal, the sale of surplus or underutilized assets was considered. The OC Fair & Event Center was included as an underutilized asset. The Orange County community strongly protested this proposed sale of the property and initiated an effort to save the OC Fair. In July 2011, two years after the proposed sale, Governor Jerry Brown halted the sale, keeping the OC Fair & Event Center as a state-owned community asset.

That same year, in a departure from past precedent, officials in 2009 dropped the practice of embracing a farm-related motif and sought to cultivate an aura of grandeur with the theme "Think. Big." As the *Orange County Register* reported, "To those counting down the days until 'Weird Al' Yankovic's triumphant return to stage at the 2009 OC Super Fair, well, there's good news and bad news. Let's get the bad news out of the way: 'Weird Al' won't be playing again until 2010 when his new album comes out. The good news, loyal legions, is that your curly-haired parody pusher will be at the fair in spirit and in mind. Take that mind part literally." "Al's Brain" was the first exhibit to use the space that would soon become the new $9 million Hangar Building the end of the fair's Main Mall. A theater built inside, dubbed the Brainitorium, is where five hundred viewers at a time enjoyed a 3-D tour through the human brain featuring Yankovic as the bizarro tour guide.

In 2010, after a year of political wrangling, the future of the Orange County fairgrounds and its annual fair remained uncertain. Officials picked a theme that reflected continuity amid uncertainty: "The Beat Goes On." This year, the Hangar Building fully debuted with its fifty-foot-tall arched ceiling and aviation hangar-style design located in the center of the property in the Main Mall. The Hangar was the stage for free community entertainment in the day and hit tribute and original bands at night like Wild Child, Hotel California and others. This year at the fair, the deep fried Klondike Bar was introduced, and a popular "Forever Fair" history exhibit dedicated to the Orange County Fair was unveiled.

The 2011 fair marked a new high for attendance with 1,401,267 guests; the fair was themed "Let's Eat!" and focused on one of the top reasons for attending the fair: the food. In addition to the usual giant turkey legs and barbecue, fairgoers were also treated to fried Kool-Aid. The 2011 OC Fair went out with a *munch*, a *moo* and an *oink* and set a record-breaking attendance. The OC Fair saw a 21 percent increase over the previous year's highest attendance record of 1,154,969, surpassed on day twenty (August 11) of the twenty-three-day event. The 2011 fair was held from July 15 to August 14.

"My belief is the 2011 edition of the fair establishes that the OC Fair has perfected the formula for staging a successful fair," said Dr. Steven Beazley, OC Fair & Event Center president and CEO. "That formula will now be applied to educate and entertain our community for years to come."

Fairgoers took the theme "Let's Eat!" seriously and consumed 10,000 Mexican funnel cakes, 3,000 chocolate-covered corn dogs, 125,000 balls of deep-fried Kool-Aid, 10,000 slices of deep-fried avocado, 2,000 deep-fried frog's legs and 75,000 colossal turkey legs.

The top five attended concerts in the Pacific Amphitheatre, in order of attendance, were Big Time Rush/Avery, Selena Gomez & the Scene, Weezer, Blake Shelton and Bob Dylan. Overall, there were nine sold-out concerts in the fair's premier entertainment venue.

In the Action Sports Arena, the most thrilling events, in order of attendance, were the Orange Crush Demolition Derby, Motorhome Madness Demolition Derby and X-treme Freestyle Moto-X.

The top shows in the Hangar were Sweet & Tender Hooligans (a tribute to Morrissey and the Smiths), Moonwalker ("The Reflection of Michael Jackson"), Journey Unauthorized, Which One's Pink? and Dead Man's Party (a tribute to Oingo Boingo).

Here are some more fun numbers for the 2011 OC fair:

- 1,000 twelve-inch-high jumbo Mexican funnel cakes were eaten, and only four fairgoers met the challenge to consume one by themselves.
- 284,982 visitors bore the cold visit into the Ice Museum, and more than 350 three-hundred-pound blocks of ice were used to create its contents.
- More than 20,733 people were "the ultimate fairgoers" as holders of their own Super Pass (season pass), compared to 11,100 in 2010.
- 32,439 people took advantage of the free Opening Hour on July 15, compared to 25,461 in 2011.
- 3,668 exhibitors submitted 12,697 entries that received 4,195 award ribbons and won more than $30,065 in cash awards.
- A total of 540 livestock exhibitors presented 3,190 animals, received 2,170 ribbons and were rewarded $30,065 in cash awards.
- For the four "We Care Wednesday" community donation drives, 81,267 generous fairgoers donated 85,000 pounds of food, 62,736 children's books, 100,000 pieces of clothing and 100,000 new school supplies.
- Born into the Centennial Farm family this year were two piglets and four goats.

"Home Sweet Home" was the theme for 2012. This year, the Pacific Amphitheatre Summer Concert Series saw its top grossing season, with seven of twenty-three concerts selling out. Sold-out artists included Young the Giant/the Steelwells; Steel Pulse/the Dirty Heads; Earth, Wind & Fire; Tears for Fears; Victoria Justice/Max Schneider; Heart; and Duran Duran.

In 2013, against a fair theme of "Come and Get It," the Pacific Amphitheatre Summer Concert Series once again had a top-grossing season, with eleven of the twenty-three concerts selling out. This year, the fair also introduced OC Fair Foodies, a collection of food-related costumed characters that roamed the property and accompanying plush toys available for purchase. The Fairs Foodies included Olivia (orange), Cornelius (roasted corn), Arturo (churro), Carl (cotton candy), Spike (carrot), Mike (bacon-wrapped turkey leg), Dip (corn dog), Clemon (lemon), Scoop (ice cream cone) and Slim (slice of bacon).

Here are some fun facts from 2013:

- Chicken Charlie used 7,500 gallons of vegetable oil to fry up 24,000 bacon-wrapped pickles, 100,000 deep-fried Oreos and other wild concoctions, like 25,000 balls of his top-selling deep-fried cookie dough.
- Biggy's Meat Market sold nearly 2,000 Big Chics on a Stick and 4,500 The Big Ribs and used 13,500 pounds of potatoes for orders of giant curly fries.
- Bacon A-Fair used 20,000 pounds of bacon around turkey legs, inside chocolate, wrapped around cheesy bombs or sprinkled around chocolate peanut butter bananas.
- Tasti Chips used 23.75 tons of potatoes and 690 gallons of cheese sauce.
- Juicy's sold more than 75,000 smoked turkey legs and used 300 gallons of ketchup and 250 gallons of mustard.
- The OC Fair offered more than 640 ways for people with a competitive streak to show off their skills in baking, preserving, painting, photography and more.
- Of the 860 individual cupcakes that were brought into the fair for the popular OC Cupcake Classic on August 3, the judges had to taste 30 each, while judges of the Get Baking Cookie Contest on July 20 had to taste 28 cookies each of the 140 individual cookies brought that day.
- Judges in the numerous culinary arts contests used more than 980 tasting spoons and forks to judge cakes, preserves, salads, chili, breads and pies.

- Some 2,400 ounces of preserved fruits and vegetables were entered this year. The oddest culinary entries submitted were dried shiitake mushroom jerky, carrot cake jam and a Snickers bar fruit salad. The most unique culinary arts entries were the Hillbilly Table-Setting and the Zombie Wedding Cake.
- The Visual Arts Gallery used 3,584 nails and hangers, each, to display the many award-winning photographs, paintings and multimedia entries received this year.
- The annual junior livestock auction saw 357 entries sell for more than $255,500 to benefit the education of 4-H and FFA youth participants.
- The tallest entry in the Floral Arrangement competition was thirty-two inches, and the shortest was six inches, with the most popular flowers used in any entry being roses and carnations.
- Tomatoes were the most popular entry in the weekly Garden & Floral competitions, and the most common entry in the "Cut Flowers" category was the rose—America's favorite flower.

"Summer Starts Here" was the theme for 2014, and for many, it obviously did. The fair saw a record three days with more than 80,000 people in attendance. The highest day for this year was 84,559, on the second Saturday (which was still less than the highest single-day record of 84,895 set in 2001). Here are some fun facts from 2014:

- More than 10,000 award ribbons were won by fairgoers for baking, photography, painting, woodworking, quilting, gardening, livestock and on-the-spot contests. This year, the fair offered 2,054 unique competitions for a fairgoer to showcase their talent.
- More than 7,800 feet of table covers and 28,200 feet of drapery were used for competition galleries, shopping halls and more throughout the fair.
- In the Visual Arts Gallery, more than 487 halogen lights, and nearly 400 walls were used to display award-winning artwork.
- The Garden & Floral competition saw nearly 1,000 tomatoes entered this year, which could make nearly 40 bottles of ketchup, plus a 300-pound pumpkin, which could make 100 pumpkin pies.
- In the Special Culinary Contests held on Saturdays, fairgoers entered 260 cupcakes, 63 bowls of chili, 35 chicken wings and 95 salsas to be judged in the only live culinary arts competitions.

An aerial view of the Orange County Fair, circa 2014. *Courtesy Orange County Fair archives.*

The Millennium Barn at Centennial Farm as it looked in the fall of 2014 during the twenty-fifth anniversary. *Courtesy Orange County Fair archives.*

- The 60 entries in the Table-Settings competition featured 300 individual and correctly placed pieces of silverware.
- In the annual junior livestock auction held on July 19, youth competitors earned more than $255,000 in auction sales and add-ons.
- In the new Bakeology exhibit, Blackmarket Bakery used more than 230 pounds of sugar and flour and 360 eggs for its daily demonstration.
- More than 1,650 pounds of watermelon were scarfed down for an award ribbon during a free nightly eating contest.
- The most common entry in the Collections competition was watches and clocks, while the strangest was a collection of "found papers," including notes, lists and flyers found in random places.
- 343 arthropods called the Explorium tent home as part of the new The Good, the Bad and the Unbelievable exhibit.
- The Centennial Farm welcomed 19 piglets this year.
- Some 5,600 individual dancers, singers, comedians and performers had a moment to shine on one of the fair's free community entertainment stages.
- The national anthem was proudly sung thirty-five times during the run of the fair.
- More than 3.5 tons of clay were molded into beautiful bowls, cups and more during the daily free ceramics demonstrations in Crafters Village.
- More than 4,300 fairgoers willingly took a seat in the Pitchburst activity area in the Explorium, only to be drenched by water balloons.
- This year, the OC Fair offered fairgoers two new Fair Foodies to take home as soft toys; fairgoers also snatched up all the supplies of Slim the Bacon within the first three weeks.

As of this writing, "One Big Party" is the theme for the 125-year anniversary of the Orange County Fair. And of course it will be. Since its humble beginning in Santa Ana back in 1890, the fair has been like a party each year in Orange County. But it has also been a place to learn, grow, compete, celebrate and make memories. Here is to the next 125 years.

Chapter 11

VOICES FROM THE ORANGE COUNTY FAIR

RACHELLE WEIR, EXHIBIT SUPERVISOR

It's hard to believe that I've actually worked here at the fair for twenty-seven years now. I think I came to my first fair when I was about nine years old, when I was in 4-H. That's when I started exhibiting. So I guess the Orange County Fair has always sort of been in my blood. It's where you spend your summer. It's where you came and realized those projects that you would be planning all year. And I really dreamed about that fair all year. It's where I learned how to carve a piece of wood, something that I knew I would exhibit. There were all those fun competitions, vying for the blue ribbon. I was always pretty competitive, and I think that competitive spirit was really healthy for all of us young people that were involved in the competitions. There was always a challenge to do things better. And then there was the raising of animals. That was a big part of my life. And it was an all-year project. You would get your animal in December, mostly pigs and steers, and then we would raise them, getting ready for that fair. It was all about the junior livestock auction. That's where we would show off our work.

That's what the fair was all about back then. It wasn't about crazy food and rides. I understand why all that stuff is popular now. But for me, the Orange County Fair always comes back to the exhibiting. That's where I spent most of my time, wandering those exhibit buildings looking at the work that everybody had done. I guess the place had such a huge profound effect on my life that it's no wonder that I've worked here for so long. I'm the exhibit supervisor, and it's something I really enjoy doing. I think, as a kid, that's the dream job that I always wished for, and here it is. To oversee all the wonderful exhibits each year is really a thrill for me.

I think that's how the Orange County Fair still really connects with the community—in those exhibits. There are amusement parks all around the world we can go have fun and find that sort of excitement. And our fair definitely delivers that aspect. But I think the real heart of a county fair is in the exhibits. That whole idea of being judged by your peers, of trying to win the blue ribbon for a quilt or an apple pie—those things still mean so much to some of the people, and I totally understand that. When I design an exhibit today, I'm thinking about what it was like here as a kid and why this stuff still really matters. The Orange County Fair has touched so many lives all over the county, I think, because it's such a unique tradition. And I think the key to our longevity is that we never let anything become stale. We are always looking for new things and always looking for new experiences to present to people. You have to do that. But you've also got to have all those exhibits that illustrate and demonstrate the passion and hard work that means so much to so many people. And you've got to have those auctions to remind the next generation of where food comes from and why agriculture is so important, especially living here in California. I'm so glad I work here. I really can't imagine being anyplace else.

FRED PITTROFF

Fred Pittroff, husband of Carmel Dyer, whose "Australian Battered Potatoes" have been a fair favorite for several decades, had his own recollections:

My involvement with the OC fair started in 1956 I was fourteen years old. I was working for Dave Barham on the boardwalk in Balboa. Dave sold Hot Dog On a Stick, Cheese on a Stick, fresh lemonade and snow cones. He also had a stand at the OC Fair selling charbroiled hot dogs.

I would spiral the hot dogs for him at our summer house in Balboa. The stand at the fair was just a wooden stand with a front counter and a charbroiler in the back.It had no roof and was wide open on a flatbed trailer. He use to haul it with his Lincoln Continental. The stand was located where the hangar is now.

The next year Dave moved across the street to the corner (now outside Building 10). He built the first glass enclosed stand selling Hot Dog on a Stick, Cheese on a Stick and fresh lemonade. I worked the first year he introduced his three signature items to the fair, and I continued working for him for many years at the fair.

As time went on, I eventually built my slides and constructed a slide in at the OC Fair. The slide was used at the fair, and we also opened for the motor cycle races. The slide was moved to the Iowa State Fair due to the construction of the then Arlington Theatre.

Fred's father-in-law, Cordy Milne; his brother Jack Milne; and Harry Oxley started the short track races at the OC Fairgrounds. They built all the portable bleachers; half became permanent. They also had previously owned the race track at Lincoln Park in Los Angeles, and when this closed down, they moved the bleachers to the OC Fairgrounds.

After we moved the slide, I partnered with Roy Marriott of Costa Mesa. He owned a plastic business and made signs for my slides, made Dave's signs, lemonade jugs and also for my stands in Australia. We built a stand, selling hot fudge sundaes and hot apple sundaes. I had the stand at the OC Fair for five years before taking it to Minnesota. We were involved in a wreck, so decided not to bring the stand back.

Another great memory I have from the Orange County Fair: Sunkist used to have a commercial machine that washed oranges, squeezed them and served fresh orange juice (I believe in what is now Building #16). They would also put it in paper cartons for you to take home.

Patrick and Peggy O'Donnell, Photographers

For more than fifty years, Patrick O'Donnell has documented Orange County. He was bitten by the photography bug as a senior at Whittier High in the late 1950s, and he's had the honor of photographing many presidents, athletes and other celebrities. He became a photographer for the *Whittier Daily News* along with the *Orange Coast Daily Pilot* and at Cal State Fullerton. In particular, O'Donnell has been the definitive lens at the Orange County Fair. For more than two decades, he and his wife, Peggy, were the official photographers of the Orange County Fair. Some of their photographs appear in this book, and to sit and chat with them is to be given an all-access tour through many historic moments of the fair. With both keen eyes and sensitive hearts, the duo enthralled thousands over the years by finding and capturing many images that are both compelling and award-winning. Patrick related the following:

I was a photographer at a newspaper, and that's how they got to know me. I had started a photojournalism contest in 1978 and was working full time at the Daily Pilot *newspaper and then part-time at Cal State Fullerton. At first, we went into the fair on a limited contract. I think it was just ten days to start, and the contracts got longer as the years progressed. This was back in the mid-1980s. And it was just Peggy and me shooting, and they sure kept us busy. We ended up shooting all the way through 2007. Shooting the Orange County Fair was just so much fun, and I loved it most of all because of the people. That's the best part of the fair for me. You can always go to any carnival all around the country, and there will always be bigger ride someplace else. So it's the people that make a difference, and the people here have always been wonderful. We would shoot all the winners in the agriculture competitions and the livestock events and then feed the images to all the local papers throughout the county. It was nice. Our stories reached so many people. And remember we were not just photographers— we were photojournalists. So we looked for stories, not just pretty pictures. I remember this woman who was exhibiting one for collections, and it was all kinds of things made out of green M&Ms. That was her whole thing. Everything had to be green M&Ms. She even showed up in a green M&M outfit. It was one of those quirky stories that people just seem to love. I shot her photos and then wrote up a little story on her, and it just took off. It got printed all over the place because it was a simple and interesting story. Sometimes these things even end up on television.*

It was also interesting to go to the fair before it opened to watch people setting up all the things that were going to be judged. These were serious competitions. You had state judges who were specially trained for these events. It wasn't just like they grabbed people and said, "Okay you can be a judge." And when you got that kind of tension, it could get very intense, very dramatic, and of course that produces some great stories.

There are so many great stories in the Orange County Fair. I think my favorite one would have to be the night Johnny Cash played there back in August 1983. I was wandering around backstage around the trailers that served as his dressing room. There were some fans out front, and I met this old guy that come all the way from Wyoming. He said that about twenty-five years back, Johnny Cash come through his little town and played a show at a Kiwanis Club or something. Johnny Cash had signed a flyer for the guy back then, and he had it with him this night. And he just wanted to see if Johnny would remember it. So I track down Johnny's PR guy, and I explain this to him, then I hear a voice from inside the trailer, that classic deep voice, and it's Johnny Cash himself. "What's going on out there?" he asked. I explained it to him, and he boomed, "Let's go see this guy!" So we go see this fan who's just thrilled beyond belief. He asks Johnny if he remembers the show, and Johnny winks at me and says, "Well sure I do!" I'm not sure if he did or if he was just making the guy feel good, but it didn't matter. It was a really beautiful moment. The guy showed Johnny the flyer and wondered if he might sign it again, right next to the old signature, and Johnny was more than happy to do it. And I'm just firing away with my camera, and it's magical. And then Johnny's wife, June Carter, heard all the commotion and came out and said, "What's going on?" And Johnny explained to her and said, "Come on, June, let's go and take a picture with this fellow who traveled so far to see us." And so I took that picture. And then Johnny said to the PR guy, "You make sure this fella gets one of the best seats in the house, you hear?" I mean, that was a really special moment. And to be able to photograph it is something I'll never forget.

As far as why the Orange County Fair is still so popular, I really think it's because they never lost track of agriculture and livestock. They're still so active with the 4-H kids to have them come out to learn about agriculture, and I think that's really the heart of it all. I mean, I absolutely think it's also about wandering all those buildings to see the knitting, whittling and all kinds of wonderful things people make to come and show off and have judged. But that Centennial Farm with the animals and vegetables is really what I think it's all about.

That's the heart and soul of the fair to me.

Then Peggy related the following:

I agree with everything my husband said, and I wish I was there for the Johnny Cash moment.

We just had so many memorable days and nights at those fairgrounds. It didn't matter to us if it was a pie eating contest or pig races or chicken races or any other kind of crazy events. We were always in the thick of it looking for those pictures the told the best stories.

I'll never forget the bride and groom that were married on an elephant at the fair. Can you imagine that? Then I remember the time the fair celebrated the 100th anniversary of the Ferris wheel. If your name was Ferris, you were admitted to the fair free that day. But they had this one guy that was going to set the world record for continuous rides on a Ferris wheel. He was on there all day and night; his girlfriend eventually joined him, and then the chef from the Ritz Carlton showed up and served them both a gourmet meal on the Ferris wheel. Those were terrific and unique things to shoot.

I also remember the bug gourmet chef who cooked crickets and worms and gave us all tastes. "Great protein," he would tell us as we clicked away. In today's digital age, it's kind of hard to appreciate how we got everything done at the fair. We did all of our own printing ourselves. We were a one-stop shop. They had a little lab on-site for us to use. My husband hired a college student named Matt Brown to help us out with our printing. Today he's one of the best sports photographers in the business. We would go through thousands of sheets of paper each fair, but that was just how you did it. We wanted to control the process because we knew we could make everything as good as it needed to be. And to me it's no great secret why the Orange County Fair has been so popular for so long. Besides all the food and games, it really does come down to what makes a fair special. And that's the agriculture and the animals. I know kids learn a lot there; so do a lot of adults. It's amazing how many people are unaware of where their food comes from and why it's so important to take care of our natural resources. But you learn those things at the fair. You see it firsthand. You can smell it, and you can taste it. And if you're hired to photograph it, then all of a sudden you have an opportunity to tell some of the best stories in the world.

JIM BAILEY, FORMER LIVESTOCK SUPERVISOR

In 2014, the Centennial Farm at the OC Fair & Event Center celebrated its twenty-fifth anniversary with a private ceremony featuring special guests, an award ceremony and, of course, cute animals.

As the fair detailed in a press release, many special guests and speakers were on hand, including California secretary of agriculture A.G. Cowher Mora, Centennial Farm Foundation board of directors vice-president Lon Records and City of Costa Mesa CEO Tom Hatch, along with the OC Fair

& Event center staff and board members. Staff member Jim Bailey was recognized for his fifty-five years of service to the OC Fair & Event center during which he helped create, build and grow the farm.

Centennial Farm is a three-acre working farm created to educate youth about agriculture and its importance to daily life. Children and adults can view fruit and vegetable gardens and livestock like pigs, chickens, peacocks, llamas, cattle and goats.

Through the farm's free school tour of the ranch and its after-school program and other agricultural programs, the farm has benefited more than 1 million schoolchildren since conception.

The farm is also home to the millennium barn, a 4,680-square-foot working barn built in 2000, with a milking parlor, horse stalls, tack room, hayloft and more. Live milking demonstrations are also offered in the barn during the farm's year-round tours program, the summer OC fair and the springtime Imaginology program.

Jim Bailey's legacy at the Orange County Fair is truly something to behold. He started out there in 1959, at age thirty-one, first working as the livestock manager. But he's probably best known for Centennial Farm, which he helped found in 1989. Throughout his years at the fair, nine of his family members were eventually employed by the fair: his wife, four children and four granddaughters. Jim related the following:

It was not long after I get out of the Korean War, in about 1957, that my family and I wound up in Orange County, living in Fullerton. Soon after that, I got involved with the Orange County Fair. I had been an agriculture teacher for some time by then, and the fair was a summer job. I really liked teaching high school kids how to raise cows and pigs and plant gardens and those types of things. That was always very important to me. I think the seeds for the Centennial Farm were probably planted back there in those first years I worked the farm because I realized how important something like that would be in Orange County.

I'll never forget once the Centennial Farm opened, there was a little kid in there, and we showed him a carrot that was just pulled up out of the ground. He had no idea that that's where carrots came from. Isn't that amazing? That's why agriculture is so important to still teach kids. I grew up on a farm in Kansas, and so this is where I come from. All I learned about growing up was growing things. And it really surprises me, even to this day, how little some kids are learning in school about all this.

4-H and FFA exhibitors with livestock exhibits entered in the Orange County Fair competition. *Courtesy Orange County Archives.*

Back at the beginning, when I first came to the fair, we had to weigh all the animals and sort them into different divisions and classes. That's something I'd never done before. Weighing animals was a huge challenge because we had those old-fashioned scales—nothing digital like we have today. They were all put up on this big platform, and it was not accurate and it was really cumbersome. Today, things are much more precise.

I really loved watching my family grow up with the fair, too. What a great place for kids to learn about responsibility and hard work. That's the thing about working on a farm. You gotta have a good work ethic. There is no faking it. I was raised that way, and I think there is no other way to look at it. That's why putting up the barn for the Centennial Farm was so much fun. We made it ourselves by hand. We designed it ourselves, and it was truly built by the community. I felt really good about getting that barn built. I know that fairs have grown in a lot of ways, and there are lots of different things that attract people today. I know people like all the crazy food and the crazy rides and stuff like that, but the heart of the fair is still where the animals and the produce is at.

That's where you learn about what a real fair is all about. Any place can have rides and food. But the livestock and the agriculture is where we learn about the community. That's we learn about where you come from and what it takes to survive. That really is the most important thing.

That fair really was a big part of my life. We raised our kids on that farm, and I got to put them all through college as a result. I supported all of them and never went into debt from working at the fair, as well as being an educator. All my kids worked at the fair; I've got some grandkids that work fairs today, too. So it really is in our blood. There's always going to be a need to learn, and that's why I think the OC fair is always good to have a place in this county. There's no better place to about life than on a farm.

Thanks to Jim, Orange County has its own three-acre working farm that's open to the public every day, barring special events at the OC Fair & Events Center. The county owes a great debt to Mr. Bailey and his family, along with all of the helping hands they've had over the years.

Becky Bailey-Findley, Former CEO, Orange County Fair

I was about five or six years old when my parents moved to Fullerton. My dad started working as an agriculture professor at Sunny Hills high school, and then he also became the livestock supervisor at the Orange County Fair. My siblings and I loved going to work with him. It was just so much fun. We would get to be on the fairgrounds before the place was even open, and so we had the whole place to ourselves. There was a nearby driving range, and I remember collecting all the stray golf balls that wound up at the fair. We would ride our bikes everyplace, and it was wide open and innocent and truly fun. It was just about as safe a haven as you could have. And, of course, there were all those wonderful animals there and just the nicest people. It really was the ideal place to be a kid.

I joined 4-H when I was a nine-year-old, and I really loved that. They would also have the 4-H youth fair in the spring, which I was also involved with. There were just so many interesting things to do at the fairground. There was really a sense of community there that took me out of my neighborhood in Fullerton and into a much larger neighborhood where I could interact with all different kinds of people and see new things every day. As a child I remember being enthralled by the hula dancers that were there from Hawaii. I had never seen anything like that before. Once I got in the high school, I was placed in charge of some of the 4-H activities. In fact, I remember the day in 1969 when our astronauts first walked on the moon. I was there at the fair. And everybody was gathered around television sets. The fair was a wonderful place to celebrate an event like that but was also a very important place when you are dealing with some kind of family tragedy because you are always surrounded by caring people.

The older I got, the more involved I became with the fair. Through high school, I got more involved with 4-H, and I took on even more responsibilities. I was participating in livestock competitions, which I loved, and I also had a role with speaking engagements at the fair—that's how I would help represent the 4-H to people. For me, as a young person, it was truly a great developmental, learning and social opportunity. I had so many friends at the fair. They were kids from all over the county that I would see for just a couple of months a year. Then we would go back to our regular lives at school during the rest of the year and reunite at summertime or in spring.

How I looked forward to seeing all of those kids again. My two sisters and brother felt the same way. It was just an idyllic place to learn about life. By the time I turned eighteen, I was working full time at the fair, and so I was able to help pay for college.

I wound up with a college career in education, and in 1986, I came back to the fair as the exhibit supervisor. My main responsibility was to help coordinate all the different competitions. To this day, I think those are really the most traditional parts of the fair. And I coordinated all of that and just loved it. I really felt at home because, in essence, I had grown up there. I knew the ropes. I knew the programs. I deeply respected the culture of the fair, and it all felt very natural for me. I loved working there as an adult because it was a way for me to celebrate the excellence and beauty that the fair is all about. I also discovered how emotionally tied I was the place after having the benefit of spending my youth there.

Eventually, I would go on to become the CEO of the Orange County Fair, and that's something I remain very proud of. As to why I think the fair remains so important to so many people, I think it's pretty simple. The Orange County Fair appropriately reflects the interests and growth of Orange County. It's a reflection of the community. And the fair has been very adept at staying connected to what is important to the community and what they want to see showcased. I know there are many people like me that feel the same way. They think back to their youth, and they remember the first time they saw a real working farm or pig or cow. It's where they learned how and why things grow the way they do. And it's where they learned, first and foremost, what makes Orange County so special. I think the fair will always be an important touchstone to generations in Orange County. And I'm so glad that our parents brought us here in the first place.

It's impossible for me to walk around the fairgrounds even today and not think back to all the wonderful memories that I had growing up there. I can still hear my father's voice around the livestock pens, and I can easily picture all of my old friends and siblings growing up in that space. I want to believe that in the next 125 years, the fair will continue to grow and continue to be a mirror for Orange County. Now, more than ever, I think it's really important to remind the next generation about why agriculture and raising animals is so important. There are many more distractions today and things to compete for people's interests, but in the end, there's really nothing like a county fair to inspire imagination and remind people about what matters.

Chapter 12

SOME FINAL FACTS AND FIGURES

MUSIC AND COMEDY AT THE FAIR

From small stages to the 8,300-seat Pacific Amphitheatre, the Orange County Fair has been the stage for a variety of concerts and entertainment. Here are some of the top musical acts that have graced our fair stage:

Adam Lambert
Aerosmith
Air Supply
Al Jareau
Alan Jackson
America
Bad Company
Bad Religion
Barry Manilow
B.B. King
Bette Midler
B-52s
Big Bad Voodoo Daddy
Bill Cosby
Black Eyed Peas
Bob Dylan

Boston
Captain and Tennille
Charo
Chris Isaak
Chubby Checker
Colbie Caillat
Counting Crows
Culture Club
Daryl Hall and John Oates
Devo
Diamond Rio
Donna Summer
Donny and Marie Osmond
Duran Duran
Engelbert Humperdinck
En Vogue

Faith Hill
Fergie
Flogging Molly
Four Tops
Gallagher
Gladys Knight
Glen Campbell
Heart
Huey Lewis and the News
Jan and Dean
Jeff Dunham
Jeff Foxworthy
Joan Jett and the Blackhearts
John Legend
Johnny Cash
José Feliciano
Kenny Rogers
Kool & the Gang
LeAnn Rimes
Lee Greenwood
Lennon Sisters
Lifehouse
Linda Ronstadt
Little Big Town
Little Richard
LL Cool J
Lou Rawls
Lynyrd Skynyrd
Mariachi Sol de Mexico de Jose
    Hernandez
Marvin Gaye
Matchbox 20
Matisyahu
Melissa Etheridge
Men at Work
Merle Haggard
Michael McDonald
Monty Montana
Neon Trees

Oingo Boingo
Paramore
Pat Boone
Paul Revere
Peter Frampton
Peter, Paul and Mary
Pointer Sisters
Queen Latifah
Rebelution
Rick Springfield
Sammy Hagar
Santana
Scorpions
Seal
Selena Gomez
Sheena Easton
Sinbad
Smokey Robinson
Steel Pulse
Steve Miller Band
Styx
Sugar Ray
Taylor Swift
Tears for Fears
The Adolescents
The Beach Boys
The Commodores
The English Beat
The Flaming Lips
The Go-Go's
The Jets
The Mamas and the Papas
The Offspring
The Temptations
The Village People
Tim McGraw
Tower of Power
Train
War

"Weird Al" Yankovic

Willie Nelson

Zac Brown Band

Ziggy Marley

ZZ Top

MORE THAN JUST A FAIR

The OC Fair has offered a unique variety of entertainment beyond concerts over the years, including record-breaking Ferris wheel rides, cattle drives down city streets and beaches, pageants and more. Here's a short list of some of the special events the Orange County Fair has hosted:

- 1897: The opening day of the fair was coined "Ladies' Day," and all women were admitted free.
- 1906: The fair celebrated the completion of the Pacific Electric Railway from Los Angeles to Santa Ana with floats and various products of the county on display.
- 1922: The automobile was a featured exhibit.

Orange County Fair, August 1949. *Courtesy Orange County Archives.*

A 4-H poultry exhibitor. *Courtesy Orange County Fair archives.*

- 1936: The "Greatest Historical Parade" recounted the romantic story of California with floats and more than one thousand costumed people and five hundred decorated horses participating.
- 1950s: Special events included daily ostrich races, pogo stick races, helicopter rides and a wild animal circus.
- 1963: A newfangled push-button phone was presented by PacBell.
- 1969: A scale model of the Apollo 11 spacecraft was featured.

- 1972: The first fair stamp in the nation became a reality, and a special post office was set up at the fair.
- 1984: The fair became bigger than life when an inflatable, seventy-two-foot King Kong towered over the fairgrounds.
- 1986: An inflatable fifty-foot Statue of Liberty wowed guests, and President Ronald Reagan and Governor Deukmejian paid visits to the fair.
- 1988: Skydivers "dropped" in on opening day.
- 1991: Dr. Norm Gray, an entomologist from University of California–Davis, performed daily in the arena, covering his body with pheromones, resulting in hundreds of thousands of bees covering his body while he played the clarinet in the key of B.
- 1993: The fair marked the 100th anniversary of the Ferris wheel with a record-breaking thirty-eight-day Ferris wheel ride.
- 1994: An authentic cattle drive down Fairview Road was staged with more than 125 riders and 250 head of cattle.
- 2001: The fair introduced adrenaline junkies to the Orange Crush Demolition Derby.
- 2007: The fair showcased two cattle drives, one on the sandy shores of Huntington Beach as part of the U.S. Open of Surfing and the

A circa 1950s 4-H member and her ribbon-winning entries. *Courtesy Orange County Fair archives.*

A program from the 1949 Orange County Fair. *Courtesy Orange County Fair archives.*

other in which three hundred head of cattle were led down the streets of Costa Mesa from Fairview Park to the OC Fair

- 2008: The fair partnered with the Maloof Money Cup to offer three days of skateboarding and BMX competitions in the Action Sports Arena.
- 2009: The fair offered attendees a self-produced, interactive exhibit called "Al's Brain: A 3-D Journey through the Human Brain with 'Weird Al' Yankovic."

The OC Fair has called several cities in Orange County home over its 125 years. It started as a horse race with a few exhibits in Santa Ana in 1890. In 1911, it was moved to Anaheim and themed "Anaheim Carnival." In 1917, after the Orange County Farm Bureau was formed, the fair moved to Huntington Beach. In the 1920s and 1930s, the fair called Santa Ana and Pomona home. In the 1940s, it returned to Anaheim but took a hiatus during World War II.

In 1949, the fair found its current home at the former Santa Ana Army Air Base when the State of California authorized the purchase of the base to be utilized as the fairgrounds for the newly formed Thirty-second District Agricultural Association. In 1953, the city of Costa Mesa, which included the fairgrounds, was incorporated.

Notable Dates

The OC Fair has grown from a three-day community event to a month-long summer must-do. From 1890 through 1971, the fair was from three to six days long and was held in either the fall or the summer. By 1972, the fair had become a standard summer event and had extended its dates to include ten days of activities. For the 1987 and 1988 fairs, guests could enjoy eleven consecutive days of fun. From 1989 to 1991, they had twelve days. From 1992 to 2002, the OC Fair hosted seventeen consecutive days of events, and in 2003, it extended its dates to twenty-one days, closing on Mondays. From 2009 to today, the fair has been open for twenty-three days, closing on Mondays and Tuesdays.

The OC Fair is celebrating 125 years in 2015 with the theme "One Big Party." Since its quaint beginnings in 1889, the OC Fair has grown to a twenty-three-day extravaganza that welcomes more than 1.3 million guests every summer.

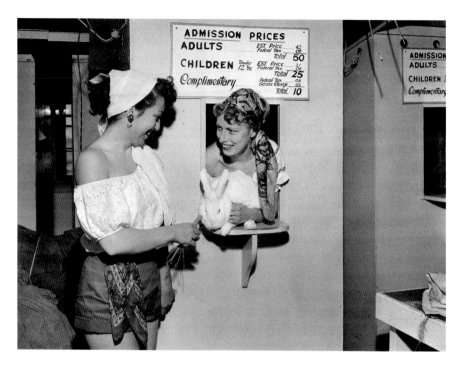

Orange County Fair ticket booths, 1951. *Courtesy Orange County Fair archives.*

Orange County Fair exhibit, circa 1954. *Courtesy Orange County Archives.*

Orange County Fair, August 1949. *Courtesy Orange County Archives.*

The OC Fair has used a variety of themes, including salutes to California produce, Orange County history and just pure fun. California agricultural industries saluted have included avocados, beef cattle, bees and honey, cheese, citrus, dairy, fiber arts, fish, fruit, gardening, gold and grain, grapes, horses and hay, insects, nuts, peppers, photography, pigs, poultry and eggs, sheep and wool, strawberries, surfing and beaches, tomatoes, vegetables and water. Following are just some of the memorable themes.

1890–1969: "Parade of Products," "Carnival of Products," "Anaheim Carnival," "Fall Festival," "Old-Time Country Fair," "Pioneer Days," "The League of Nations," "Golden Days of Montezuma," "Most Beautiful in America," "Mighty Carnival of Joy," "Kiddieland," "Carnival Getaway," "Port-O-Plenty," "Accent on Youth," "Gay '90s," "Better Living through Agriculture," "Hawaiian Holidays," "Diamond Jubilee of Country," "Yesterday Meets Tomorrow" and "Fiesta of Fun."

1970–1989: "Country Fun," "Something for Everyone," "Action '72," "Good Old Days," "The Orange County Fair Comes Alive," "Home Grown," "A Touch of Country" "There's Still a Touch of Country," "The All-American

Orange County Fair, August 1949. *Courtesy Orange County Archives.*

Orange County Fair, Rosedale Family Farm exhibit, circa 1950. *Courtesy Orange County Fair archives.*

An aerial image of the Orange County fairgrounds from the 1980s. *Courtesy Orange County Fair archives.*

Orange County fairgrounds, 1949. *Courtesy Orange County Fair archives.*

Fair," "Everything's Coming Up Rosy," "It's a Horse of a Different Color," "It's Wild and Woolly," "Jump on Over," "Don't Miss the Egg-citement," "We're Beefin' Up" and "Stop and Smell the Flowers."

1990–2015: "Very, Berry Extraordinary," "How Sweet It Is," "Meet Our Main Squeeze," "100 Years in the Making," "We're Having Bushels of Fun," "It's the Wheel Thing," "Saddle Up for Fun," "Come to Our Garden Party," "For Kids of All Ages," "Best Pickin's in California," "We're Puttin' a Bug in Your Ear," "We're Goin' Tropical," "Nuttin' but Fun," "We're in the Pink," "Join the Rush," "Hot! Hot! Hot!," "Twist & Shout," "Leap into the Fair," "Red, Ripe & Rockin'," "Jammin' at the Fair," "It's Callin' You Out to Play," "Flower Power," "CowAbunga," "Say Cheese," "Think. Big.," "The Beat Goes On," "Let's Eat!," "Home Sweet Home," "Come & Get It," "Summer Starts Here" and "One Big Party."

INDEX

A

Action Sports Arena 113
All-Alaskan Racing Pigs 107
Alyn, Kirk 95
Anaheim Carnival 135
Arlington Theater 102

B

Bailey, Jim 96, 98, 124, 126
Balboa Pavilion 21
Bill, Tiger 90
Brainitorium, the 112
Butram, Pat 81
Buttons, Red 89

C

Cagney, James 67
Carillo, Leo 50
Carter, June 122
Cash, Johnny 122
Centennial Farm 12, 98, 99, 102, 110,
     113, 117, 122, 123, 124, 125
Chapman, C.C. 43
Clark, Dick 92

Coasters, the 89, 92, 96
Crafters Village 117

D

Diamond Jubilee 79
Drury, James 86

E

Edison, Thomas 18
Ellington, Duke 81
Euroslide 107
Evans, Dale 90

F

Ferris, George W. 18
Ferris wheel 18, 33, 34, 54, 102, 103,
     123, 131, 133
Findley, Becky Bailey 96
4-H 20, 47, 49, 50, 55, 61, 67, 70, 75,
     85, 90, 104, 105, 115, 118, 122,
     126, 127
French Opera House 19
Future Farmers of America 50, 67,
     82, 90

INDEX

G

Grassroots, the 89, 92
Gray, Norm 100

H

Hangar Building 112
Harborlites 89
Harvest Home Festival 22
Hattie, Hilo 76, 77, 78
Hibbard, Preston 89
Hope, Bob 90
Hughes, Howard 68
Huntington Beach 12, 22, 23, 24, 25,
  26, 27, 28, 29, 30, 31, 32, 33,
  34, 35, 36, 37, 38, 43, 55, 81,
  89, 111, 133, 135
Husky, Ferlin 86

I

Imaginology 124

K

Kiddieland 52
Korean War 124

L

La Grande Wheel 107
Laguna Beach 96
Los Angeles County Fair 40
Los Angeles Times 12, 56, 59, 64, 68, 73,
  76, 78, 80, 98, 102

M

Macres, Harry 79, 80, 91
Maloof Money Cup 111
Marble, Robert 100
McCarthy, Robert ("Father Mac") 95
Mexican-American Day 89
Miss Garden Grove 89
Moore, Sonny 50
Mosier, Beverly 96

Motorhome Madness 113
Municipal Bowl 46, 50

N

Nelson, Ricky 91
Newport Pop Festival 82
Nike missile station 70

O

OC Fair Centennial Experience 102
OC Fair & Event Center 112
O'Donnell, Patrick 120
Orange County Association 11
Orange County Community Fair
  Corporation 19
Orange Crush Demolition Derby 107
Orbison, Roy 92

P

Pacific Amphitheatre 102, 103, 104,
  105, 108, 113, 114, 129
Parade of Products 21
Philbin, Regis 89
Pirate Queen 76
Pomona 40, 41, 46, 47, 135

R

Reagan, Ronald 133
Righteous Brothers 96
Rogers, Roy 90

S

Santa Ana 11, 12, 19, 20, 21, 23, 38,
  40, 41, 46, 50, 55, 73, 76, 117,
  131, 135
Schubert, Yvonne 68
Sea Dragon (ride) 95
Silkwood 19, 20
Smithsonian Institution 96
"Star-Spangled Banner, The" 86, 117
Statue of Liberty 95, 133
Superman 95